# COACHING FOR STAFF DEVELOPMENT

## Angela Thomas

Personal and Professional Development

# COACHING FOR STAFF DEVELOPMENT

## Angela Thomas

*Management Consultant*
*Third Eye Training Limited*

 Published by The British Psychological Society

First published in 1995 by BPS Books (The British Psychological Society),
St Andrews House, 48 Princess Road East, Leicester LE1 7DR, UK.

A catalogue record for this book is available from the British Library.

ISBN 1 85433 155 8 paperback

Typeset by Gem Graphics, Trenance, Mawgan Porth, Cornwall
Printed in Great Britain by BPC Wheatons Ltd, Exeter

# Personal and Professional Development

SERIES EDITORS:

Glynis M. Breakwell is Professor of Psychology and Head of the Psychology Department at the University of Surrey.

David Fontana is Reader in Educational Psychology at University of Wales College of Cardiff, and Professor Catedrático, University of Minho, Portugal.

The books in this series are designed to help readers use psychological insights, theories and methods to address issues which arise regularly in their own personal and professional lives and which affect how they manage their jobs and careers. Psychologists have a great deal to say about how to improve our work styles. The emphasis in this series is upon presenting psychology in a way which is easily understood and usable. We are committed to enabling our readers to use psychology, applying it for themselves to themselves.

The books adopt a highly practical approach. Readers are confronted with examples and exercises which require them to analyse their own situation and review carefully what they think, feel and do. Such analyses are necessary precursors in coming to an understanding of where and what changes are needed, or can reasonably be made.

These books do not reflect any single approach in psychology. The editors come from different branches of the discipline. They work together with the authors to ensure that each book provides a fair and comprehensive review of the psychology relevant to the issues discussed.

Each book deals with a clearly defined target and can stand alone. But combined they form an integrated and broad resource, making wide areas of psychological expertise more freely accessible.

OTHER TITLES IN THE SERIES
*Interpersonal Conflicts at Work* by Robert J. Edelmann
*Managing Time* by David Fontana
*Effective Teamwork* by Michael West

# ACKNOWLEDGEMENTS

I should like to express my thanks to Colin Monks for his many useful suggestions for this book from his vast knowledge of and experience in management training. In addition, I would like to record my debt to participants on my coaching courses for their comments and support. I am also grateful to Dr David Fontana for his helpful comments on the whole manuscript.

# Contents

# DEDICATION

To Colin, Jennifer and Sam

# *What Is Coaching and Why Is It Important?*

It is commonly accepted that coaching is one of the most important ways in which managers stimulate the development of their staff. Effective coaching is a 'must' if the organization is to get better results year after year and if the manager is to make a difference in the performance of the staff. If you have not coached before, many new experiences await you. Coaching has its highs and lows, but if you are well prepared, they can be mostly highs. Managers who are also successful coaches help their subordinates master new skills and techniques: they model the skills needed for success and feel good about themselves in the process. Coaching is communication: successful manager coaches are also skilful communicators and motivators. This is an enormous challenge. Good intentions are not enough: you will need all your knowledge and skills in order to be successful. This book will help to give you a firm foundation to acquire this knowledge by teaching you more about the skills of successful coaching. Most managers have learned some skills of coaching through years of trial and error. This book will shorten this learning process, and reduce those painful errors, by drawing upon others' good experiences.

But *Coaching for Staff Development* is only one source of information. Another way you can learn about coaching is to observe and talk to other managers who coach, but they can teach you both effective and ineffective practices. Of course, another important way to learn is from your own experiences as a practising coach when you can examine these experiences periodically and think about what you are doing: what you can do differently to coach more successfully, and what you want to repeat because it has worked well.

It won't take long to read *Coaching for Staff Development*, but it may take some time to digest its contents, and perhaps even longer to put into practice what you learn. You may need to read and re-read parts of this book, practise the skills described, and learn from the experience through thoughtful analysis. As you undertake this study, you will realize that successful coaches are those who learn new skills, who are flexible enough to change old ways when change is required, who can accept constructive criticism and who can evaluate themselves.

*HOW DOES THIS BOOK WORK?*
You will find a mixture of things in this book. Obviously the main text is designed to inform, to provoke, to pull things together and to give you ideas for further study. There are two other ways in which information is presented. The checklists contain additional information which is not crucial to the main flow of ideas but which, rather, is intended as illustration. Read these or skip them as you wish while going through each chapter. The second is the series of exercises which are intended to make the learning personal and to give you the opportunity to use your past experiences to improve your present coaching practices. (These are positioned in the text according to the issues they centre on, but it is recommended that you set time aside after reading either the whole of the chapter or the section of the chapter in which they are placed to complete them.) They are designed to make the book both a guidebook and personal exploration.

*A WORD ON TERMS*
Different words are used in various work environments – in both the public and private sectors of industry and commerce – to describe relationships of authority or of hierarchy. Support personnel may be described as 'staff', 'colleagues', 'employees' or 'subordinates'. Those higher in the hierarchy may be referred to as 'supervisors', 'bosses', 'superiors' or 'managers'. I propose to use the terms 'subordinate' and 'manager' as my research indicates that these are the ones most frequently used in industrial and professional life in the majority of cases.

# THE PRIMARY AIM OF COACHING

Before giving my favourite definition of coaching from the many available, I would first like to set the scene. The idea of coaching came originally from the world of sport, where an instructor would try to get the best possible performance from an individual or team without themselves taking part in the physical action. Most top sports people are quick to credit the role their coaches play in their success – and in professional life it would be nice if people could say the same of their managers. Whenever I have discussed this analogy on training courses, however, it has been met with rueful laughter. This is because although it would be perfectly normal to go to one's tennis coach and say, 'I have a problem with my back hand. Can you watch me in action and work on it with me?', people find it hard to conceive of going to their manager with an equivalent request.

There are both 'selfish' and more altruistic reasons in favour of coaching. Selfish, because if a manager can get subordinates to a level where they can do work with less supervision, or do work which at the moment demands managerial attention, then the manager will be able to spend more time on more strategic tasks such as long-term planning, or product and market development. Less selfish reasons are where there will be significant benefits to the organization as well as to the professional development of the subordinates themselves if effective coaching is encouraged.

Coaching helps subordinates use their work as a guided learning experience. They thus learn by doing, as well as via feedback from the manager. Through good coaching, the aim is to help subordinates to generate knowledge and experience themselves, rather than being force-fed knowledge and being exposed only to vicarious experience.

Coaching is a much underrated management skill. It has a major part to play in achieving results through other people. The aim of the ideal coaching situation is to allow the subordinate to complete a task the manager has assigned, while at the same time strengthening the subordinate's skills ready to take on the responsibility for that and similar assigned tasks in the future.

The aim of coaching, therefore, is organizational excellence through the effective use of everyone's abilities and potential, in a way that allows growth in knowledge and experience.

## WHAT ARE THE BENEFITS OF COACHING TO THE ORGANIZATION?

Coaching brings direct benefits to the organization, but perhaps more significantly, it brings a range of benefits in the form of better working practices on the part both of managers and of subordinates. These practices involve enhanced teamwork, increased creativity (the realization that there is not just one way of doing things), freer communication, and a reduction in crisis management. Overall, coaching allows the manager to change from management to leadership. After an initial investment of time, the manager is therefore able to take on more challenging assignments. This is clearly of great benefit to the individual manager, but there is also a significant potential gain in the quality of output of the organization. The motivational impact of coaching is likely to lead to a smoother-functioning department, and to an increased understanding of work roles.

Subordinates are also likely to be clearer about goals, and will show greater readiness and willingness to achieve significant results. This growth in competence is of benefit to the talent pool of the organization, and recognition of success after good coaching should also lead to an upward spiral where the confidence inspired will lead subordinates from success to success. This does not happen automatically. Clearly, before the upward spiral begins, other conditions must be present.

## THE CONDITIONS FOR EFFECTIVE COACHING

Effective managers get work done largely through others, and thus the ability to coach is one of the most important skills in the job. Coaching is a challenging task because it involves the manager in sharing tasks, recognizing any fears about coaching they may have, developing an effective coaching style, and helping subordinates to develop and take on new challenges. For a coaching programme to be done effectively, the following conditions are necessary:

- an open and trusting climate
- a helpful and empathic attitude
- a non-threatening atmosphere
- a collaborative, one-to-one dialogue
- a focus on work-related goals, a review of progress and feedback on behaviour
- an enhancement of understanding of the work environment

- a focus on the subordinate's strengths and areas for improvement

- an identification of any problems that hinder progress and achievement of goals

- provision of the support required to enable the subordinate willingly to take on responsibility and authority for delegated tasks.

## SETTINGS GOALS AND OBJECTIVES

One of the more critical conditions is the focus on goals and it is worth looking at this a little more closely. Goal-directed behaviour is normally more efficient and more effective than behaviour which is spontaneous, unplanned and unorganized. Explicit goals help to describe the purpose of the task, help gauge performance, identify the next steps to be taken and highlight any behaviours that need to be changed. Effective goals must be future-oriented (what will be seen, heard and felt when they are achieved), clearly and un-ambiguously communicated, realistic, achievable and challenging, actionable (within the area of responsibility and authority given), and measurable in terms of whether the subordinate has reached the standard set. In a coaching programme the manager determines the overall aim, objectives and goals for the task in hand. This is done in conjunction with the subordinate at the beginning of coach-ing sessions so that the agreed outcomes become part of the sub-ordinate's perception of the task to be achieved, helping them to have a greater degree of involvement, appreciation and ownership of the task. Coaching is an essential first step on the road to the significant process of delegation.

## DELEGATION

Delegation, defined simply as the assignment of responsibility and authority to another, is an integral part of any manager's job. Delegation has also been conceptualized as a time-manage-ment tool, a decision-making process and a way of getting more things achieved through others. Of course, different managers have different views of delegation based on their perspective of people and on their management philosophies. For example, one manager may see delegation as a means of influence, control and personal power, while another may use delegation as a way to gain trust,

## ATTITUDE TO COACHING

### EXERCISE 1

If I am honest with myself, I believe that:

1. Coaching takes more time and patience than it is worth.

   Yes ..................... Maybe ..................... No .....................

2. If I coach, I give up too much control.

   Yes ..................... Maybe ..................... No .....................

3. Coaching involves too much risk – I have taken a long time to acquire my skills and expertise. No one can do the job as I can.

   Yes ..................... Maybe ..................... No .....................

4. I'll look bad if one of my subordinates fails.

   Yes ..................... Maybe ..................... No .....................

5. I enjoy my job and I am reluctant to hand over bits of it.

   Yes ..................... Maybe ..................... No .....................

6. My subordinate is a specialist and doesn't see the whole picture.

   Yes ..................... Maybe ..................... No .....................

7. I am concerned about what will happen to me if someone else successfully takes on a bit of my job.

   Yes ..................... Maybe ..................... No .....................

**Review**

*Yes:* If you have answered yes to any of these questions, you may have a problem in your attitude to coaching. Please think about your reasons and maybe even discuss them with a colleague whom you trust. You should also read the appropriate sections of this book carefully.

*Maybe:* Try to identify the reasons for your doubt and review them. Look at the appropriate sections of this book and concentrate on the positive aspects/benefits of coaching.

*No:* Fine! You have a good attitude to coaching. Read on and improve your coaching practices.

commitment and loyalty from subordinates. How the manager manages will reveal much about what he or she delegates, the quality of the subordinates being coached and the professional development that results.

The benefits of delegation seem to outweigh the potential drawbacks, yet many managers are hesitant to delegate in spite of the fact that a wide range of tasks can be delegated; only the responsibilities that demand the manager's personal attention, such as the handling of a performance problem, or duties inherent in the manager's job, should not be delegated.

## Reasons for not delegating

- a belief that coaching takes too much time, planning and patience
- the desire to maintain authority and control
- a lack of confidence in the subordinate's competence
- the manager's belief that they can do a better job
- a perception that the job is too important to take risks
- the manager's enjoyment of doing certain tasks personally
- the belief that subordinates are specialists and don't see the whole picture
- the manager's concern for visibility from upper management
- the fear that the subordinate may do a better job
- the manager's belief that he or she does not have the skills to coach.

Delegation within the coaching process employs the same management skills to organize and distribute the workload in an effort to maximize the usefulness of available human and technical resources. So what are the skills of delegation?

## The skills of delegation

- setting goals and objectives
- enhancing individual abilities, confidence and initiative
- recognizing and praising good performance
- encouraging increased commitment and motivation.

However, the manner and style in which the delegation is done is important: usually, the whole task is given to the subordinate, who is left to get on with the job. This can be a risky business unless learning is highly valued and understandable mistakes are accepted. In a coaching programme, the manager assigns just part of the task until he or she is happy that it has been done satisfactorily and then proceeds to assign other bits until the whole job can be delegated. In this way the subordinate feels a sense of involvement, gains increased confidence, competence and motivation. The manager withholds full authority and responsibility from others until all parts of a particular task are achieved and the subordinate has had time to practise with hands-on experience and is willing and able to take on that responsibility.

## THE LINKS BETWEEN COACHING AND DELEGATION

Perhaps it's more a question of the progression from coaching to delegation rather than the links between them. In many ways the two are trying to achieve the same end, and certainly use some of the same methods. Equally, both demand a significant amount of time if they are to be done properly. There are, however, some important distinctions between the two processes.

The first of these is that coaching tends to be specific to a situation. The time frame is relatively short, and the coaching is carried out with a very specific end in view. Delegation, by contrast, is likely to be longer term and more generalized, aiming at a more permanent change in activities. Secondly, coaching can help the subordinate to undertake only part of an assignment, whereas delegation tends to relate to the whole assignment. Thirdly, the primary focus of coaching is on learning and development, whereas that of delegation usually focuses equally on learning and development and also on getting the job done. Coaching should therefore precede total delegation of a task. And finally, delegation tends to lead to a change in job description whereas coaching is concerned with the job as it currently stands.

Coaching provides a route for the rapid transfer of skills, knowledge and experience from one person to another in an on-task – and therefore relevant – job setting. In addition, coaching is a flexible tool. Not every athlete can aspire to an Olympic gold medal – but all can aspire to working at the best of their ability. There is room for silver and bronze medals and also for those who are unplaced. Coaching is a way of getting people to perform to the best of their ability, whatever that ability is. It provides for learning through a process of discovery, through discussion, and through hands-on experience. The end result of good coaching is the successful completion of a task delegated by the manager, together with a strengthening of skills, knowledge, motivation and self-confidence.

## COACHING ROLE MODELS

### EXERCISE 2

1. When did you have a period of rapid growth and learning in your career? .................................................................
...........................................................................................

   What happened to promote this? .........................................
...........................................................................................
...........................................................................................

2. (a) Who was your manager at the time? .........................
...........................................................................................

   (b) What was your working relationship like with this person? .........................................................................
...........................................................................................

   (c) What did they do to further your growth? ....................
...........................................................................................
...........................................................................................

3. What effect did the things you have written have on your professional self-concept and motivation to work?
...........................................................................................
...........................................................................................

4. What guidelines for you, as a coach, can you identify from your experiences? ...............................................................
...........................................................................................
...........................................................................................
...........................................................................................
...........................................................................................
...........................................................................................
...........................................................................................
...........................................................................................

# WHY IS COACHING NOT MORE WIDELY USED?

In professional life the word coaching is more common than the act, and is often used for something which can best be described as 'poor delegation', of which more later. Many professionals concede that they receive day-to-day guidance and help from their managers, but complain that it is neither structured nor systematic. Why is this? Why do some managers seem reluctant to coach their subordinates? One of the reasons is that they have few role models to follow, and may not consciously be aware of what good coaches in the past have done for them. A useful preliminary exercise, therefore, is for managers to focus on the time in their jobs when they felt most stimulated and most encouraged in professional growth. They can then focus on their senior manager at that time in order to identify role model behaviour – and perhaps identify that good coaching involves not just a set of techniques but also personal qualities such as empathy, trust, integrity and a willing-ness to have confidence in subordinates. These qualities are rarely found in managers who assert that subordinates should find their own way, and who complain of lack of time.

Some of the reasons for the absence of good coaching lie with subordinates too. When given new tasks to perform, subordinates may feel unwilling to admit doubt or ignorance of the best way to proceed. They will struggle, sometimes under great stress, to work out how to approach the task, how to get information and develop options, and may spend considerable time on endeavours which do not contribute to the actual objective, when all that was required from the manager was a minimum of guidance, instruction, demonstration, opportunity to practise and feedback. Coaching, as we have seen, is about learning, but needs a longer-term view. There are shorter-term learning approaches too, which have a different impact.

*MISSED, WASTED POTENTIAL*
There is nothing intrinsically wrong in the time-honoured way of learning a job – traditionally described as 'sitting with Fred or with Nellie'. Especially today, however, where we face considerable pressure to perform quickly and efficiently, sitting with these venerable folk is often a time-consuming way of learning, depend-ing as it does on the (often untrained) coaching skills of Fred or Nellie. Of course, more sophisticated methods can be seen as a threat to insecure subordinates who may be reluctant to

ask questions, to expose uncertainty or any lack of knowledge, and things can be made worse by a manager who is not gifted with social skills and professional understanding. Regrettably few managers are really in touch with what their subordinates are doing or with their capabilities. Research done by Yankelovich (1983) into the work and human values of the non-managerial work force showed three important findings:

1. Less than one in four job holders say they are currently working at full potential.
2. Half said that they did not put effort into their jobs over and above what was needed.
3. Seventy-five per cent said that they could be significantly more effective than they currently were.

Yankelovich called this the 'commitment gap'. Also, the response of subordinates to the researcher's question, 'Would your boss notice if you put 10 to 15 percent less effort into your job?' is usually, 'No!'

Effective motivation in professional life and in the workplace involves offering that little bit extra that cannot be commanded. Subordinates will only do optimum work and use the large amount of discretionary time they have, if they are motivated to so. Coaching is an effective way not just of helping subordinates to learn their jobs better, but also a way to generate commitment to producing challenging results and, at the same time, to improve the relationship between manager and staff.

### Differences between coaching and on-the-job training

| *Coaching* | *On-the-job training* |
| --- | --- |
| • aims at future performance – longer-term orientation | • aims at current performance – 'now' orientation |
| • emphasis on learning | • emphasis on performance |
| • linked to potential | • linked to performance |
| • stretches performer to new limits | • consolidation within current limits |
| • focuses on whole assignment | • focuses on specific activity |
| • based on dialogue | • didactic |
| • explores new material | • uses known material or extends it |
| • high risk. | • low risk. |

WORK-RELATED STRESS

Lost productivity on the scale suggested by Yankelovich is, to say the least, a worrying factor for managers. It is, however, only part of the story. According to recent research, stress is costing the UK 20 million pounds per day in lost production at work (Gregory, 1994). Stress is brought about when people face more challenges than they can cope with. The term stress is limiting because it describes both a condition and a cause. It focuses attention on the worst of times and on weakness. In today's hard-driving and thrusting business world, there are increasing numbers of casualties through work-related stress which affects health and home life (Fontana, 1989) and which causes some to reconsider their careers (Cooper *et al.* 1988). The findings were surprising in that so many managers were willing to admit to the strains and pressures of their working life. Responses to these pressures determine not only the quality of lives and the quantity of work achieved but also the very survival of the organization itself. However, many individuals and organizations do not believe that stress should be a major concern because they simply do not see the problem. Stress is in the eye of the beholder, and what one person sees as stressful, another may see as a challenge; what can frighten one person can thrill another.

Handy (1988) points out that definitions of stress vary in the way in which they combine individual and environmental factors but 'they all centre on the stressed individual and then either work backward to analyse the causes of stress or forward to investigate the individual's response to stress'. Examples of this include Cooper's (1988) work, where stress is understood to be a response to internal or external processes which reach levels that push physical and psychological capacities to their limit and beyond. The cognitive theory of stress and coping by Lazarus (1966) emphasizes that people respond to threatening or challenging situations according to their perceptions of them and their coping mechanisms. These models are valuable in focusing on the psychology of the individual but this is often at the expense of paying attention to the structures of organizations which constrain people to think and act in particular ways. Karasek's (1979) model of stress, derived from empirical research in the work-place, postulates that psychological strain results from the joint efforts of the demands of a work situation and the control available to the worker facing those demands. This effectively recognizes the

## THE MANAGER AS COACH: STRESS TENDENCY TEST

### EXERCISE 3

Rarely true (A)   Occasionally true (B)   Almost always true (C)

...........    1. When I coach I worry about making mistakes.

...........    2. My workload makes me feel too overloaded to coach.

...........    3. I worry that others are not going to do the job to my high standards.

...........    4. I am on edge when I coach.

...........    5. It would upset me if my subordinates were to criticize my coaching.

...........    6. Before a coaching session I am very nervous.

...........    7. I find the coaching situation overwhelming.

...........    8. As a coach, I feel I want to control everything.

...........    9. I tend to find the bad things someone else does first.

...........    10. I tend to fly off the handle when a subordinate makes a mistake.

...........    11. When I coach I worry about losing respect.

...........    12. When I coach I worry about subordinates making serious mistakes.

...........    13. When I coach I do not feel adequately valued for my abilities and commitment to work.

relationship between the subjective experience of stress and the social conditions which may give rise to it. The most stressful jobs are those with high demands combined with low discretion (control). This dual concept of control and responsibility is crucial to coping with stress and developing well-being. Research indicates that while responsibility is indeed an important ingredient in stress, control is the balancing factor. Cooper *et al.* (1988) have identified and located occupational stress in five categories. These are factors related to the job: noise, lack of privacy, shiftwork and boredom; the role of the individual in the organization (for example, when given conflicting tasks to perform or insufficient information to carry them out); social relationships and interpersonal demands; prospects for promotion and advancement; and the organizational structure and climate. Manifestations of stress may include job dissatisfaction, mental ill health, heart disease, accident occurrence, alcohol-related and social/domestic problems. The importance of how different sources of stress combine and have a cumulative effect has been more widely recognized in recent years.

Work-related stress is more likely in an atmosphere of distrust, hostility, lack of social and other support, and lack of communication. Unclear job specifications and descriptions can also add to a feeling of vulnerability – as well as making it difficult to assign priorities and allocate appropriate amounts of time to each task. But what has all this to do with coaching? Personal experience has indicated that only after successful coaching are subordinates likely to be able to give accurate descriptions of the jobs they are employed to do. Research has consistently shown that managers and subordinates often have very different views of the tasks of the latter. Managerial stress is often generated by the pressure to achieve results, often in a short time-frame. Self-doubt may exacerbate the situation, as may feelings of impotence in the face of poor performance by subordinates. For the subordinate, stress can arise from an awareness of managerial dissatisfaction, together with the fear of highly visible failure. The subordinate who feels that this manager is creating stress by an inappropriate management style and who reacts through complaining, taking time off or living in fear, is responding in ways that are unhealthy not just for the individual but for the organization. The subordinate who takes responsibility for talking about the problem with the manager has plenty of freedom to respond in healthy ways.

Stress, of course, is not always negative in its consequences. It can provide challenge and encourage creative and effective thinking as long as it's not excessive. A little stress keeps our mental muscles toned and ready for action and the adrenalin is as beneficial to us as it is to someone playing sport. But more stress than 'just enough' can impair performance. So how can good coaching help to reduce stress? Five major principles can be followed to reduce stress both in managers and subordinates. These are:

- the specification of results and not methods,

- accountability given to the subordinate, with the manager avoiding intervention,

- the manager being available when needed,

- positive feedback by the manager, and

- the identification of learning points from failures.

We will return to these points in later chapters.

### How coaching can reduce stress in the long term

- The manager is available to give guidance – the subordinate no longer feels alone and can cope with new tasks.

- The subordinate has a greater sense of control as goals and measurements are more clear.

- The challenge of being coached for new performance ensures that boredom has no place.

- Coaching establishes an atmosphere of trust, co-operation, support and clear communication between manager and subordinate.

- Misunderstandings about the nature of the subordinate's job are clarified and dealt with.

- Mistakes are viewed as learning experiences.

## THE DEMANDS ON THE MANAGER AS COACH

There is, of course, considerable stress on the manager once he or she starts to coach. A major aspect of this is borne out by the general lack of information lower in the organization – information is often seen as a form of power. McNeil (1993) asserts that the increasing integration of innovative information technology into business will have important consequences for company culture. With information at their fingertips, subordinates will be in a position to take more and more decisions for themselves. At that point, each organization has to weigh up how much authority it is prepared to allow them – whether it wants so many subordinates to be decision-makers. Clearly 'empowerment' must be tempered with practicality. What will happen to middle managers when responsibility for many decisions is passed down to their subordinates? The answer, according to McNeil, is that the manager's role need not become redundant but will have to be adapted. Managers will have to learn to play a 'coaching role', passing on their experience and ensuring teams work to common goals.

So, what demands does coaching make upon the manager? Coaching is a demanding helping profession, and the better the manager's mental and physical condition the better able they will be to help others. Again, coaching is a potent strategy for building commitment. It thus goes beyond the normal management function of clarifying direction, accountability, responsibility and performance standards. It demands also that the manager has a real concern not only for results but also for people. There are specific demands made of the manager if successful coaching is to take place. One of them relates to 'hard' management skills, and concerns the need for good communication. The others are all in the 'softer' areas of self-awareness and awareness of the needs of others. For several reasons, successful coaching managers must have self-confidence and must:

- Be willing to relinquish aspects of their own responsibilities (what John Cleese has called 'growing up') and should not feel challenged by questions – not always as easy as it might sound.

- Maintain an open mind – the subordinate will perhaps challenge some long-held assumptions.

- Be prepared to stay out of the situation once the task has been delegated, and be able to view mistakes by subordinates as a way of learning, discussing these subsequently in a positive, learning-oriented way.

Some managers might find it difficult to accept these points. They might ask why management techniques that seem to have worked perfectly well in the past have to be changed. The answer lies in getting and keeping a competitive edge. Those organizations in which decision-making power is delegated to subordinates, who are often closer to the 'action' than managers, will react more swiftly to clients' wishes. Managers often have to accept that they should open up their organizations and departments and not be afraid of surrendering some of their power. But even visible organizational benefits may not be enough to persuade some managers to adopt a different approach. Stereotypically, British, French and German managers are seen as being averse to change, and to resent any upheaval or diminution of managerial power. This reluctance will need to be overcome if organizations are to develop management structures and cultures capable of quick response to change.

There are two others areas of knowledge which benefit the coach. The first is knowledge of personality styles, which helps with effective communication. The second is a knowledge of different learning styles, which means that methods of communication will be relevant. If the manager's own 'learning profile' differs markedly from that of the subordinate, learning is more difficult, less comfortable, and may even not take place at all. The issues of personality and learning styles will be returned to later, in Chapter 2.

The final demand is on the manager's time – from two perspectives. First, the manager's own time. Planning for the coaching sessions, performing the skills involved, allocating space for reviews and checking on progress all take up time. Many managers argue that it is quicker to do tasks themselves than to spend so much effort coaching others. However, this may be true the first time and possibly the next, but in the long term it certainly is not.

Secondly, the manager needs to realize that the subordinate may take longer to do the delegated tasks. The subordinate is at the beginning of a learning experience and is not as skilled as the manager. It is fatally easy for managers to begin to display impatience, which may panic the subordinate, destroy self-confidence and possibly trust. A realistic review of the time needed to perform the task by someone with a less developed level of skill should therefore be discussed during the initial coaching sessions with the subordinate. This chapter has outlined a way in which that process might be initiated.

In conclusion, coaching is a vital skill that managers need to learn and practise. Its popularity comes at a critical time against a background of rapid technological change, recession and redundancies – a time when companies and other organizations are slimmer than ever and have to meet, even exceed, customer expectations. Reversing the trend of employee dependence, lack of commitment, and increasing the trend towards subordinate empowerment, are progressive moves in line with today's need for a quality-oriented business environment. Resistance to coaching needs to change if staff are to feel accountable, to grow, and to experience success in the job. The end results of good coaching are greater commitment to helping the organization achieve its mission, an enhanced climate of professional excitement and energy, and an achievement-orientated environment which releases potential.

To summarize:
❑ Coaching aims at organizational excellence through the effective use of everyone's abilities and potential, in a way that allows growth in knowledge and experience.

❏ Coaching benefits the organization through increased productivity: it benefits the manager by allowing them to spend time on higher level tasks; it benefits the subordinate by helping them to grow and succeed.

❏ Coaching is a crucial skill for managers, but many conditions need to be present before it can be done successfully.

❏ Goal setting is vital. Goals should be future-oriented, well-communicated, achievable and challenging.

❏ Coaching is a significant first step on the road to delegation and shares many of the same skills. Coaching, however, tends to be more specific than simple delegation; it has a shorter time frame, has a very specific end in view and aims more at development.

❏ A good role model in the manager's past experience can be helpful in clarifying the impact of personal qualities (empathy etc.) as well as techniques.

❏ Motivation is about that little bit extra that cannot be commanded. Not everyone, however, works to full capacity and effectiveness.

❏ Stress also contributes to a loss of effectiveness, and can stem from the job itself or from the environment of the job.

❏ Good coaching can have a marked effect on the reduction of stress in the work-place.

❏ Coaching changes the relationship between manager and subordinate. It helps to achieve the balance between concern for results and concern for people.

❏ Good coaches have a mature view of themselves and their responsibilities and have confidence in their subordinates.

❏ As information and decision-making power flow further down organizations, coaching is a vital tool to ensure that organizations develop structures, cultures and abilities to respond more quickly to change.

# Chapter Two

# *Personality Factors and Other Obstacles to Coaching*

## NEGATIVE ASPECTS OF COACHING

As we have seen, coaching is not an easy skill; there are factors which can be intimidating for both manager and subordinate. A major factor which can make or mar coaching lies in the personal compatibility (or clash) between manager and subordinate. Some of these aspects are discussed in this chapter, along with guidance on assessing one's own personality type as well as those of subordinates.

### *UNCLEAR ROLE*
Although coaching can be seen as an important management tool, there is often little clear understanding of exactly what it involves in the way of skills and activities. In addition, there may be no clear understanding of whose responsibility it should be. The manager may not have a thorough understanding of what to coach, when to coach or how to coach. There may be uncertainty about how much guidance, direction and socio-emotional support is needed, or even whether subordinates would be ready and willing to accept help. The overall result may be that the manager fails accurately to evaluate the present or potential performance of a subordinate for any given task.

### *INAPPROPRIATE MANAGEMENT STYLE*
Management style is the consistent behaviour pattern that a manager uses when working with, and through, other people. Managers develop habits of action that become somewhat predictable to those who work with them, and they may be afraid

that these habits will be changed or eroded in the coaching situation, giving feelings of insecurity to all concerned. Confidence in subordinates is often influenced by the manager's assumptions about human nature; the amount of control or freedom the manager gives to others often depends on whether he or she believes that they are basically lazy, unreliable and irresponsible, or alternatively are creative, self-motivated and likely to show initiative (McGregor, 1960). Subordinates will, of course, vary in the extent to which they want strong leadership as well as in the extent to which they show independence or dependence, initiative and creativity. Managers may thus need to adapt and modify their behaviour and their beliefs about people if they are to be successful in the coaching process. What managers expect from subordinates and the way in which they treat them largely determine progress and performance. Coaching intensifies this close relationship between the manager and the subordinate and the behaviour and expectations of both – which can cause a great deal of strain.

## DIFFICULTIES WITH DIRECT PERSONAL CONTACT

Coaching involves managing by direct personal contact. This contact can sometimes be difficult for a manager who is unused to being in a one-to-one relationship with a subordinate for any length of time. The manager may fear loss of privacy in getting too near to someone else physically or emotionally. There may be a fear that the situation will show up deficiencies in technical knowledge or expertise. And there may also be a fear of the loss of perception in others of their personal power – the resource that enables a manager to gain compliance and commitment from subordinates. The manager too could fear an actual loss of personal power – in how their subordinates respect and are loyal to them. In addition, the manager may exercise too much 'position power' in the coaching situation so that they become overbearing and encourage dependence rather than independence. The subordinate could react by showing lack of initiative, lack of response and common sense, or by not voicing suggestions or creative ideas. This could result in turn in the manager becoming frustrated and enforcing ideas as to how a task should be performed, or even solving a problem personally rather than facilitating learning in another. This 'disempowerment' (missing the opportunity to develop competence) robs the subordinate of the opportunity to grow in confidence, self-reliance, independence and experience.

# WHAT IS YOUR MANAGEMENT STYLE?

## EXERCISE 4

*Place yourself on this continuum*

1. Are you primarily negative or positive in the messages you deliver?

   Negative .............................................................................. Positive

2. Do you give judgemental or constructive feedback?

   High in judgement ................................................... High in information

3. Are you a good listener or do you interrupt and talk too much?

   Poor listener .................................................................... Good listener

4. Are you consistent in your communication and in giving feedback?

   Inconsistent .......................................................................... Consistent

5. Are you aware of the non-verbal messages you convey and how they can destroy or enhance your communication with others?

   Unaware ....................................................................................... Aware

6. Do you communicate clearly and directly or do you communicate in abstractions?

   Indirectly and unclear ............................................. Clearly and directly

7. Do you catch people doing right and reward them or do you catch them doing wrong and punish them?

   Focus on mistakes ----------------------------------- Focus on successes

8. How much interest and concern do you show in the growth of your people?

   Little ............................................................................................. A lot

9. Do you encourage people to think for themselves or do you usually provide the answers?

   Provide answers ...................................................... Encourage thinking

## INADEQUATE COMMUNICATION SKILLS

Written and oral communication skills are critical in the coaching situation. The manager's success or failure as a coach depends upon their ability to make thoughts, feelings and needs known. They should also be generally receptive to attempts by the subordinate to reciprocate in kind. The manager who tends to be verbose and gives sketchy instructions and explanations will confuse rather than enhance communication, and could cause the subordinate to take decisions without being in possession of sufficient facts. The manager may be unable or unwilling to disclose any personal experiences or knowledge that might help the subordinate to learn (and thus enhance their perception of what the manager requires) more accurately.

## LACK OF WILLINGNESS

A subordinate has to be ready and willing to accept the manager as coach. Both have to regard coaching as a process of encouragement and growth aiming at the development of skills in a particular area of work. If this willingness on both sides is not apparent, stress and anxiety, withdrawal, resentment or other clashes can manifest themselves. Unless the manager gives the reason for the coaching session – i.e. problem-solving, development to take on more responsibility, a shortfall in performance – the subordinate may regard the coaching session as a confrontation, a reprimand, or even as harassment. This situation can arise whether the subordinate is older or younger than the manager, or particularly if they are lacking in confidence, or have low self-esteem or a negative image of themselves.

## LACK OF MOTIVATION

When a manager is asked if they think they are good at coaching, the general reply is 'Yes, I believe I am.' However many of the participants on my courses think differently about their bosses. One replied; 'Any relationship between what I thought my job responsibilities were, and what my manager thought they were, was purely coincidental!' As a result some subordinates are motivated to do good work and others are not. This difficulty may arise because the motivational tools chosen do not match the needs of the individual concerned at that time. The manager as coach has the additional job of creating a motivating environment for the subordinate, but with organizations down-sizing and jobs disappearing or being integrated, it is becoming harder to do. The subordinate's professional allegiance is more likely to have first call on personal loyalty rather than on the organization. Markham (1993) states that, in future, people will describe their jobs primarily in terms of their activities rather than in terms of their employment. Motivation is therefore likely to derive more from acquiring and mastering new knowledge and skills, opportunities for decision-making and involvement, rather than from promotion up the management ladder.

## PRESSURES IN THE JOB

Managers give many reasons why they are not motivated and are hesitant to coach. They may feel their organization has a 'do-it-yourself, that's what you're paid for' attitude. Or they may feel it takes too much time to coach, and that a project can be too complicated to explain to someone else who does not have the manager's experience and expertise. Ultimately the problem could be one of perfectionism: 'I was recruited for my expertise in this area, and my superiors could think I'm shirking my responsibilities if I delegate my work'.

Another difficult area concerns fear of failure if the subordinate does not do well, or, conversely, insecurity if the subordinate outshines the manager. Or the problem could be workaholism: the manager thrives on pressure, and feels threatened, stressful and guilty if tasks are relinquished to others.

## MAKING MISTAKES

Whereas it can be beneficial sometimes to make errors and learn from them, managers and subordinates share a fear of making and admitting mistakes. Consequently they may go to enormous lengths to hide them, whereas if they were admitted early on, much time and effort would be saved. Building up trust in the coaching relationship could obviate this situation.

## DIFFICULT SUBORDINATES

Subordinates who behave unwillingly or ineffectively can benefit from feedback from managers. Feedback provides information to the subordinate on how things affect the manager, and used properly, can be a helpful control mechanism to help the subordinate change their behaviour. The manager can then use the problem-solving nature of constructive discipline as a learning process which provides the subordinate with an opportunity for positive growth. Sometimes, however, the manager will be faced with renewed aggression or hostility from the subordinate as a result. If the manager feels frustration and hostility in turn, this could prevent any new and more desirable responses being made use of. There could be feelings of hurt when the manager is doing his or her best to develop the subordinate and might reasonably look for appreciation and support. Hostility can be exhibited in a variety of ways. An angry subordinate can hurt or undermine the manager's job and reputation through gossip and other malicious behaviour, or may look for a scapegoat as a target for hostility, or forget to do a task, or even cause deliberate damage.

*ALL IN ALL*

Questions of role, style, personal contact, communication skills, willingness, job pressures, fear of mistakes and difficult subordinates – this is a daunting list of potential problems! Each of these, with good coaching, however, can be turned into real improvement opportunities both for relationships and for productivity. It may take some courage to coach for the first time – but many things are frightening the first time, like speaking in public, or abseiling. The first step is the most difficult, and as with many activities, good preparation is a key. The rest of this chapter will focus on some of the thinking to be done prior to a programme of coaching.

# COACHING FROM THE MANAGER'S PERSPECTIVE

Management has been defined as the process of 'working with and through individuals, groups and other resources to accomplish organizational goals' (Hersey and Blanchard, 1988). The success of any department within an organization depends on the development and performance of all its staff rather than solely on the personality of the manager. If each member of that staff is to be empowered to take on more responsibility for what they do, the manager's role thus becomes more demanding. The manager will have to switch from managing by control to managing by commitment – from themselves and others – and finally to managing by operating as a facilitator in a learning partnership. The manager who wishes to accomplish this should see the coaching process as a vital tool towards meeting the challenges and choices inherent in new situations, ensuring that others are ready and willing to take on responsibility and authority for tasks delegated when required to do so.

It is, therefore, important that managers gain commitment through allowing others to have increased responsibility, increased involvement in key decisions affecting them and their work, and increased opportunities for creativity and entrepreneurship. This mobilization of creative energy becomes even more important to the manager. Coaching is as much to do with how things are done as with what is done and thus inevitably involves patience and commitment on the part of the manager. Measurable changes in the learning and application of new skills take time to inculcate and develop. Managers need considerable flexibility and adaptability to deal with the different personalities and priorities that confront them: leading and facilitating become critical skills. Coaching is successful for the manager when improved performance can be observed – when other people have the ability to accomplish tasks more successfully and take on assigned responsibility and authority.

## COACHING FROM THE SUBORDINATE'S PERSPECTIVE

Many of the jobs done by support staff have changed significantly in recent years. Generally, people are more skilled and better educated than before and are more interested in the quality and meaningfulness of their work than was previously the case. But if a department is going through a process of change, many subordinates will experience alternating periods of confidence and doubt, having a significant effect on motivation and morale. They are likely to feel 'switched on' when objectives, goals and procedures are clear, and 'switched off' when there is inconsistency and confusion and no obvious picture of the road ahead.

However, a high proportion of subordinates receiving coaching rate their managers highly. They feel that coaching is a powerful and relevant tool in learning to take on the responsibility and authority for new tasks, to have the opportunity to question and test assumptions, and to develop more appreciation for the problems and pressures the manager experiences. They perceive coaching to be a distinct and separate set of skills, very different from the normal management ones, and a set that every manager should learn.

For the subordinate, coaching is successful when growth is achieved personally and professionally through the manager's encouragement, support and guidance. Coaching for the manager is successful when a particular person's improved performance can be observed through their ability to accomplish the tasks more successfully and take on delegated responsibility and authority.

## COMPATIBILITY BETWEEN MANAGER (AS COACH) AND SUBORDINATE

Coaching is successful when it results in the achievement, maintenance or improvement of a positive working relationship between the manager and the subordinate, who should be compatible in many ways in order to achieve a trusting and working relationship. In other words, a level of comfort has to be achieved and maintained for both to stay focused on the task or problem in hand without having to puzzle out what is going on. Sometimes two people are psychologically or temperamentally incapable of working together, and conflict results. In order to succeed and have a greater understanding of these manager-subordinate interactions, the manager needs to have some under-standing of personal strengths and weaknesses, of the differences and similarities in terms of personality or behaviour between the two of them.

# PERSONALITY VARIABLES IN MANAGER AND SUBORDINATES

Everyday in the work-place a manager faces the potential for success or conflict in dealings with subordinates and in maximizing the efficiency and productivity of the department. Every individual has tendencies and natural preferences to behave in certain ways. For example, one subordinate may measure success by results and will do whatever it takes to get the task done. Another will place high value on recognition and measure success by the amount of praise and acknowledgement received. Another may strive for a secure, stable and predictable environment and will avoid any sudden, unplanned changes that upset equilibrium or cause stress.

Another may have a tendency towards perfectionism in checking and re-checking processes and procedures while complying with established rules and regulations.

There are more than a dozen varied models of behavioural differences, but they all have four main categories in common. Most focus on internal characteristics leading to external behaviour. In 1923, Carl Jung developed one of the most comprehensive theories to explain human personality. Where other observers saw people's behaviour as random, Jung saw patterns. What he called 'psychological types' are patterns in the way people prefer to perceive and make judgements. In Jung's theory, all conscious mental activity can be classified into four mental processes – two perception processes (sensing and intuition) and two judgement processes (thinking and feeling). Jung influenced a number of subsequent personality trends, one of which led to the Myers-Briggs Type Inventory (Lawrence, 1979), and another to the work of Marston (1928) and later Geier and Downey (1989). Both trends produce personality theories which yield four main sets of characteristics which can be combined into 16 main personality types or styles based on patterns of observable, external behaviours. This latter is the model to be discussed here.

## FOUR BEHAVIOUR TYPES

This model is simple, practical, easy to use and remember, and divides people into four core behavioural types. The following is an overview of these types: *the dominant directive type, the interacting socializing type, the steady relating type and the cautious thinking type.* Of course, most people are a mix of these, falling into one of 16 styles, and each presents the manager with different problems in the coaching situation.

### THE DOMINANT DIRECTIVE TYPE

Dominant directives are driven by an inner need to lead and be in personal control, and to take charge of people and situations so that they can reach their goals. They are problem-oriented and enjoy a challenge: are outspoken, controlling, strong-willed, independent, restless, goal-oriented, given to challenging people and conventional practices and dislike routine. They have a high level of confidence, a good self-image and high ego-strength. They dislike personal exploitation (especially being taken advantage of) and personal weakness and may go to extremes to avoid situations involving either.

Their approach to problem-solving is pragmatic, reactive, decisive and competitive. They strive to feel important and impress others with their workloads, efficiency, persistency and single-mindedness. They like opportunities to complete tasks in a creative manner, but can sometimes be over-focused on results instead of on the means towards them, and this achievement-orientation can manifest itself in a tendency to over-work. Dominant directive individuals often prefer strong, directive management, but can work quickly and impressively by themselves.

The less positive attributes of this group include stubbornness, impatience and toughness. Naturally preferring to take control of others, dominant directive individuals may have a low tolerance for the feelings, attitudes and inadequacies of others. Under pressure, they are likely to vent their anger by ranting, raving or challenging and blaming others. They naturally react to tense situations with a fight response, regardless of others' views and feelings, and also tend to be selective listeners.

## Coaching dominant directive types

- Show them how they can win; give them new opportunities.

- Vary the routine and look for opportunities to introduce variety.

- Display reasoning and logic, and develop their listening skills, for instance, by getting them to paraphrase everything agreed.

- Provide concise data, facts and highlights.

- Agree on goals and boundaries, get verbal acknowledgement as well as clear closure and commitment at the end of discussion – with written documentation if necessary – then leave alone (though with support).

- Allow them to exercise initiative within appropriate limits.

- Increase their awareness of the consequences of jumping to premature conclusions.

- Notice and compliment them on their *accomplishments* (not personality).

- Let them take the lead, when appropriate, but provide them with relevant parameters.

- If necessary, argue with conviction and assertiveness on points of disagreement, but on the basis of facts and not of personality.

- Help them to become more aware of others' feelings and the benefits of developing more satisfying relationships.

## THE INTERACTING SOCIALIZING TYPE

This type is talkative, popular, persuasive, impulsive, enthusiastic, energetic, needs to be socially recognized and likes to be treated with warmth. The interacting socializer tries to influence others in an optimistic, friendly way focused on positive outcomes, whether in a social or work environment. Admiration and acceptance from others means more to this type than to any other. Since recognition and approval motivate, this type often likes to be in the limelight and near the hub of activity. The biggest fear for people of this type is public humiliation or enforced isolation – whether as a result of being overlooked or of being thought unattractive, unsuccessful or unacceptable. Public humiliation threatens their core need for approval, and they may go to extremes to avoid it.

In the work situation their approach to problem-solving is supportive, trusting, instinctive, exploring and appeasing. They like to brainstorm and interact with colleagues, enjoy freedom from control, details or complexity, and like being a key part of an exciting team and being included in important projects, activities and events. Their natural weaknesses are over-involvement, impatience and short attention spans. They can be bored easily, tend to make sweeping generalizations on the basis of minimal data, and may neglect to check things. When they experience insufficient stimulation and involvement, they become bored and seek variety. When taken to the extreme, these behaviours can lead to superficial, erratic and overly-emotional behaviour. There may be a tendency towards poor time-management skills, particularly an inability to set limits on telephone calls, drop-in visitors, meetings and routine tasks.

## Coaching interacting socializing types

- Support their need for approval and appearances by being enthusiastic and showing trust and support for their ideas and feelings whenever possible.

- Avoid complicated details, and provide a 'holistic' focus.

- Display reasoning and logic, and help them to develop listening skills by prompting them to paraphrase everything agreed.

- Help them develop a plan for achieving results on a consistent basis and to refrain from losing sight of goals or setting unrealistically high expectations.

- Support their need for involvement and contact by interacting and participating with them, but set time limits on discussions and tasks.

- Vary the routine and avoid long-term repetitive tasks.

- Provide them with genuine appreciation, drawing attention to their accomplishments and progress.

- Participate with them in tasks (as they often need help in getting organized) and coach them in logical decision-making processes so that their ideas can be turned into results.

- Act non-aggressively, and avoid personal arguments as they dislike conflict.

- Give action and stimulation by keeping up a fast, lively pace, but at the same time help them to identify the pros and cons of the situation.


*THE STEADY RELATING TYPE*
Individuals of this type are usually calm, measured, easy-going, predictable and modest. They prefer a slower and easier pace than the other types, favouring steadiness and a tendency to follow-through actions. They focus on building trust, and aim for long-standing personal relationships. Their goal is to maintain a stable, secure, balanced environment. They are pleasant and co-operative, and seldom incorporate emotional extremes such as rage or euphoria into their behaviour.

Generally, they fear sudden changes, and are concerned with outcomes; they need to think and plan for changes. Any disruption in their routine can cause distress. More assertive types may take advantage of them and of their tendency to capitulate and avoid confrontation. Their reluctance to express themselves can result in hurt feelings.

Their problem-solving approach to daily work is through observation, reflection, application and implementation. They like to know the order of procedure, and prefer to be motivated by familiar and proven practices. Steady relaters dislike risk, and favour repetitive tasks; they may avoid uncertainties by maintaining the status quo. They also respect tradition, demonstrate loyalty, gravitate towards relationships that provide security and are uncomfortable with conflict or confrontation. These types have patience, staying power, persistence and commitment. They enjoy setting and implementing established guidelines and assembling equipment, and prefer to start work only when everything is ready and in place. But they have high perseverance and stick to a project for relatively long periods of time or until concrete results are produced. They are accommodating, and like to get along with others through predictable role relationships.

## Coaching steady relating types

- Explain how your ideas will minimize risks.

- Give adequate advance warning of any changes or new, unstructured assignments or untested techniques.

- Convince by reasoning and logic and provide necessary data and proof.

- Demonstrate interest in them.

- Provide clear outlines and instructions.

- Compliment their steady, persistent behaviour and patience.

- Act non-aggressively towards them; focus on areas of common interest, and avoid conflict.

- Allow them to provide service and support for others.

- Provide a relaxing and friendly working environment.

- Acknowledge their non-combative manner and co-operative behaviour, and provide feedback at appropriate times.

*THE CAUTIOUS THINKING TYPE*
Cautious thinkers' strengths include accuracy, dependability, independence, care and resourcefulness. They tend to be private people, to be non-disclosers – both of thoughts and emotions. They are contemplative, introverted and reflective, and ponder 'Why?' as well as 'How?' in situations. They are inventive, like to see things in

new ways, often have a unique perspective, and are low risk-takers, but they can appear aloof, introverted and insensitive. Generally they fear uncontrolled emotions and irrational acts, and these traits may impair goal achievement. Similarly, they fear emotionality and irrationality in others, strive to avoid embarrassment, and may over-control both themselves and their emotions.

When problem solving, cautious thinkers analyse, evaluate, plan and investigate before acting. They prefer tasks to people, they like clearly-defined priorities and prefer to know the pace required, especially where deadlines are involved. They often focus on expectations and outcomes in regard to policies, practices and procedures. They are concerned with process and will want to know how things work so they can evaluate them correctly; by virtue of their need to be right, they prefer to check results for themselves. They tend towards perfectionism, which taken to extremes, can result in 'paralysis by over-analysis'. They have a natural inclination to validate and improve upon accepted processes, and often find new ways of viewing old questions, concerns and opportunities. But their overly cautious traits may result in worries that the process is unsatisfactory, which further promotes their tendency to behave in a critical, detached way. Due to compliance to their own personal standards, they demand a lot from themselves and others. However, they often keep their criticisms to themselves and share information, both positive and negative, only on a need-to-know basis when they are assured that there will be no negative consequences for themselves. They reject aggression but can be assertive when they perceive they are in control of a relationship or their environment. Having determined the specific tasks, margins of error, and other variables which will influence the desired results significantly, they will take action. However, they can be slow to reveal certain concerns or problems, because they always need additional factual information to put things into perspective.

### Coaching cautious thinking types

- Approach them in an indirect, non-threatening and careful way.

- Show the reasons for decisions and provide explanations and rationale.

- Allow them to think, enquire and check out others' progress and performance before they have to make decisions.

## BEHAVIOURAL TYPES

### EXERCISE 5

(a) *dominant directive type*    (b) *interacting socializing type*
(c) *steady relating type*    (d) *cautious thinking type*

1. Think of specific individuals you manage who represent each of the four main behavioural types.

    (a) ...............................................................................

    (b) ...............................................................................

    (c) ...............................................................................

    (d) ...............................................................................

2. How can you apply what you have learned about the four main types to improve your working relationships with each one?

    (a) ...............................................................................

    (b) ...............................................................................

    (c) ...............................................................................

    (d) ...............................................................................

3. List some of the characteristics that work to the advantage of these different types of people in their job performance.

    (a) ...............................................................................

    (b) ...............................................................................

    (c) ...............................................................................

    (d) ...............................................................................

4. Which characteristics work against them?

    (a) ...............................................................................

    (b) ...............................................................................

    (c) ...............................................................................

    (d) ...............................................................................

- Compliment them on their thoroughness and correctness when appropriate.
- Ask for clarification and assistance to avoid conflict and defensiveness.
- Allow them time to contemplate, reflect and find the best or correct answer within available limits.

## ADAPTABILITY IN THE COACHING SITUATION

It will be helpful to the manager as coach to gain an increased understanding of the natural differences between these types in order to gain some insight into their behaviours at work. Adaptability on the part of the coach is the key to success here – it requires the willingness and ability to engage in a range of behaviours not necessarily characteristic of a manager's particular style in order effectively to deal with a situation or relationship. Adaptability should be evident in the manager's attitudes and involves making strategic adjustments to their methods of communicating and behaving, in response to the particular needs of the relationship. This way, the manager can treat others in the way they want to be treated. For example, as we have seen, dominant directive individuals are task-oriented, fast-paced, decisive and seek power and control, whereas cautious thinkers are task-oriented, slower-paced, deliberate, and seek accuracy and precision. Interacting socializers and steady relaters are people-oriented and slower-paced, but the former seek popularity and prestige and are spontaneous, while the latter seek sincerity, appreciation and agreement. Adaptability does not mean imitation of that person's behavioural style: it means maintaining your own identity but with changes in behaviour (speech style, feedback and so on) to suit the other person.

**Action plans for interacting with the four main types**

Dominant directive types
- Get to the point quickly and decisively.
- Avoid getting bogged down in minute details.
- Operate with conviction and don't bluff.
- Know what you are doing.

| | |
|---|---|
| Interacting socializing types | ➤ Show energy and liveliness. |
| | ➤ Focus on the give-and-take of interaction. |
| | ➤ Make the encounter fun and enjoyable. |
| Steady relating types | ➤ Cultivate a casual, easy-going relationship. |
| | ➤ Deal one-to-one with them. |
| | ➤ Treat them with warmth, feeling and sensitivity. |
| Cautious thinking types | ➤ Use an orderly, logical, accurate approach. |
| | ➤ Focus on process and procedures. |
| | ➤ Give well thought-out and accurate documentation. |

## THE MOTIVATING ENVIRONMENT

As the manager's style meshes with that of the subordinate (i.e. with communication flowing effectively), motivation at an enhanced level becomes possible. Motivation is the energizer of behaviour. Motivational states result from the multiple interactions of a large number of variables, among them the need or drive level of the person, the incentive value of the goal, the person's expectations, the availability of the appropriate responses (i.e. the learned behaviours), the possible presence of conflicting or contradictory motives and, of course, unconscious factors.

People are driven by different motives at different times. Determining which motives are affecting behaviour at any particular time is complicated by the fact that motives vary in strength and importance, the most powerful one at the time guiding behaviour. In other words, motives are hierarchical, and as they vary from individual to individual, with different priorities and even different hierarchies, determining a good management style is difficult. Furthermore, motives are normally invisible – even the individual may not be aware of their real motives – and so the only way to discern them is through the individual's overt behaviour, which places a high premium on the manager's skills of observation and empathy.

Work is, of course, a major source of motivation, with both organizations and employees having expectations of each other –

from the relatively simple economic ones to more complex psychological contracts involving such aspects as commitment and willingness to take or to give responsibility and autonomy. For the employee, the way the organization (through its managers) fulfils expectations is the key to satisfaction and motivation; it also has a major impact on self-esteem. The assumptions that people develop about themselves are largely shaped by the explicit and implicit views that managers and the organization have about their own values, goals and methods: matters such as how information (and what information) is communicated, dress codes, the messages communicated by office layout, space, even window access – are examples of how these are expressed.

## MODELS OF MOTIVATION

Management theorists have developed many models – some more complex than others – to help in the understanding and the management of motivation. The following models offer a broad view of possible factors which a manager should find useful in the coaching situation. They show the range of variables which might account for people's motives in the work place:

1. The **'rational-economic'** model, held by Taylor (1947) and expressed by McGregor's (1960) Theory X and Y. Theory X states basically that most people have to be coerced into work by economic incentives and require constant management supervision. Theory Y postulates that people can be self-directed and creative at work if properly motivated.

2. The **'social'** model formulated by Mayo (1933) through the Hawthorne experiments, which recognized needs other than economic ones and stressed the importance of a worker's peer group on performance.

3. The **'self-actualizing'** model which understands the needs of the individual to develop full potential (Argyris, 1957) and recognizes the difference between attitude and behaviour. McGregor's Theory Y postulates that people can be self-directed and creative at work if properly motivated. Herzberg's (1966) 'motivation-hygiene' theory concludes that people have two different categories of need that are essentially independent of each other, and which affect behaviour in different ways. Maslow's (1970) 'hierarchy of needs' shows that the behaviour of individuals at a

particular moment is usually determined by their strongest need.

4. The '**complex**' model (Schein, 1991) argues that in the huge gamut of human needs and motivators, an individual's response will be governed by many variables at different times and in different situations.

While the underlying motivations each individual may bring to the work environment are indeed influenced by many variables, there is a 'hierarchy of needs' which can be identified:

### A hierarchy of needs

| | |
|---|---|
| Safety and security | ➤ Leads to management practices aimed at making tasks predictable with little risk or uncertainty. |
| Affiliation | ➤ The manager can motivate subordinates with this need by providing opportunities for interaction with others on team projects and assignments. |
| Esteem | ➤ The manager can satisfy this need by giving recognition, feedback and appreciation for work well done. |
| Power | ➤ The manager can give increasing opportunities to influence decisions and to direct projects. |
| Achievement | ➤ The manager can satisfy this need by giving subordinates new and challenging tasks to stretch and test abilities, exercise their talents and make success achievable. |
| Autonomy | ➤ As the subordinates move towards greater freedom and independence in the job, the manager reduces the closeness of supervision and encourages them to set their own work schedules. |
| Self-actualization | ➤ The manager gives more and more challenging work and allows creative expression. |

The manager as coach has to rely on the support and co-operation of subordinates to achieve success and must also see subordinates as potentially competent to take on assigned (and eventually delegated) tasks. In this chapter we have discussed the factors involved in coaching. Chapter 3 goes deeper into what the coaching process actually is.

To summarize:

❑ Management style is the consistent behaviour pattern the manager uses when working with others.

❑ Subordinates vary in the type of management style they respond well to – the amount of control or freedom expected, for instance.

❑ There are many other difficulties in the coaching situation: e.g. direct personal contact, inadequate communication skills, lack of willingness, lack of motivation, pressures in the job, fear of making mistakes or difficult subordinates.

❑ Coaching can provide an opportunity to improve on these problems. A shift in management style, however, may be needed to gain commitment and to mobilize energy.

❑ Subordinates who receive good coaching rate their managers highly.

❑ Compatibility between manager and subordinate is important in the achievement of a good working relationship. An understanding of personality is needed for this.

❑ According to research stemming from Jung, there are four main personality types – the dominant directive type, the interactive socializing type, the steady relating type and the cautious thinking type. All four have very different personality characteristics and need to be handled differently in a coaching situation. Adaptability to deal with each is a key to success.

❑ Motivation is a further critical factor and depends on many different variables. Four models which affect the way the manager views subordinates are: the rational economic; the social; the self-actualizing and the complex.

❑ Individuals are driven by different motives at different times. Motivators are hierarchical, individualistic and invisible and therefore can only be inferred by the manager.

❑ Needs fit into a hierarchy, moving from needs for safety through affiliation, esteem, power, achievement and autonomy to self-actualization.

# Chapter Three

# *The Nature of Successful Coaching*

The definition of coaching used throughout this book is that successful coaching is a system of staff development which allows the subordinate to learn by a process of discovery, through guided discussion with the manager and through hands-on experience. It involves the manager and subordinate in a one-to-one dialogue following a structured process which leads to renewed commitment to sustained improvement and superior performance in the subordinate, and to a positive working relationship with the manager.

## COACHING AS A LINE PROGRAMME

For the manager as coach to play the appropriate role and communicate effectively, a structured plan of action is needed. The manager has to offer expertise and subject knowledge in their own field, but at the same time must present and develop these skills in a way which facilitates learning for the subordinate and which is professional. They should also motivate, listen and provide feedback on the work as well as recognize and reward work well done. David Kenney, Management Development Manager for 2,000 Boots stores says: 'we emphasize that it is fundamentally the manager's responsibility to coach, but historically, only some of our managers accept this and even fewer do it. But attitudes are changing and it is part of my mission to ensure that 100 per cent of our managers behave as good coaches'. (Parsloe, 1992)

These managerial functions of planning, organizing, motivating and influencing are central to the coaching process. Planning involves setting goals and objectives for those tasks for which the subordinate will assume responsibility in the future. Organizing involves the development of 'work maps' showing how goals are to be accomplished, as well as the organization and integration of resources to attain the goals. Along with these, creating a motivating environment plays a significant part in determining what levels of work a subordinate may aspire to, which in turn influences how efficiently and effectively the goals and objectives of the task are met. In this way the behaviour of the subordinate is channelled towards achieving the results required, using strategies skilfully for mutually rewarding and productive purposes. In order to be a good coach, therefore, the manager needs a variety of skills, and the experience to know when to use them efficiently and effectively. Research has found that hourly-paid employees could hold on to their jobs by working at only 20 to 30 per cent of their ability. However, employees work at close to 80 to 90 per cent of their ability if highly motivated; if motivation is low, the employee's performance will suffer as much as if ability is low. It is clear, therefore, that the manager's role as a coach is a vital one.

Learning to be a good coach involves learning by doing, rather as in sport. How does one learn to hit a golf ball for example? The only way is by standing on the tee and attempting to hit the ball, and by practising over and over again until one succeeds. No manager will be a good coach merely by wishing to be, by reading about it or by watching a video. These methods will, of course, increase the motivation, but will provide only conceptual knowledge about coaching. Learning involves a more or less permanent change in behaviour – that is, being able to achieve something different from what one was able to do before. In reading and watching others perform, all the manager acquires is, at best, a change in knowledge or attitude. If you want to learn to be a good coach, you have to 'take a stab at it'; in other words, practise so that the process becomes part of your managing behaviour.

Of course, for all the reasons discussed in the previous chapter, you as a manager might feel anxious and a little uncomfortable because you are changing your habitual behavioural pattern. You have to go through this 'unfreezing' to learn a new behaviour pattern. The probability of getting things right first time with so many individual differences in working style is low and the temptation to revert to old, comfortable ways of behaviour will be strong. With perseverance the new style will lead to greater success in terms of people's motivation and increased performance. It is necessary to recognize that if you are to hit the golf ball correctly and consistently more often, it takes practice.

## DIFFERENCES BETWEEN COACHING AND COUNSELLING

Coaching is centred on the organization and department rather than on the individual, i.e. the organization is the main beneficiary. The duty of the manager as coach is to promote the organization's welfare by identifying and correcting performance shortfalls and problems, or by coaching other people to take on more responsible tasks. In counselling, the client (usually the subordinate) is the main recipient; but here it is the client's and the counsellor's joint responsibility to promote the well-being and welfare of the client. Furthermore, coaching is initiated by the manager more often than by their subordinates: it is the manager who decides that the person needs a new skill, new knowledge, has a performance shortfall to correct, or needs to take on a task with more responsibility. In counselling, on the other hand, the client is the one who seeks out the counsellor (who will not necessarily be the manager) because of a personal, an attitudinal or a behavioural problem which the client cannot cope with or solve by themselves.

Coaching is directive whereas counselling is non-directive. The manager as coach usually decides what to talk about and leads the subordinate in a pre-determined direction, encouraging them to offer ideas and opinions. In counselling, there is no pre-conceived idea as to where the discussion should lead: in fact, the counsellor follows in the direction the client wants to go. Coaching is objective as opposed to subjective. In coaching, the feelings, aspirations, values and motives of the subordinate, though important, are secondary to the main objective, which is to improve performance or results. A good coach, therefore, is objective and impartial, focusing on the problem to be solved, the task to be learned, the development to be achieved and the responsibility to be transferred, rather than on the specific needs of the individual. On the other hand, to be effective, the counsellor must, before all else, gain the respect and trust of the client (this is of course also important in the coaching situation), but in addition needs to show positive feelings towards the client as a person, to be empathetic, warm, friendly and non-judgemental, and to accept the client's values, goals and interests as being legitimate.

*TO SUMMARISE – COACHING OR COUNSELLING?*

| The manager as coach | The manager as counsellor |
|---|---|
| Identifies performance deviations and determines the causes of the deviations. | Helps the subordinate to work through a personal problem. |
| Motivates the subordinate to correct the deviations by using improved knowledge, skills and application. | Is sympathetic, supportive and non-evaluative. |
| Teaches new knowledge and skills to the subordinate. | Serves as a mirror and a sounding board for the subordinate. |
| Actively helps the subordinate to solve problems and to use creative ideas for the improvement of processes and procedures. | Acts as a resource for the subordinate, when needed by them. |

| Coaching is | Counselling is |
|---|---|
| Organization-centred; the organization is the main client. | Individual-centred; the subordinate is the client. |
| Initiated by the manager; the manager decides that the subordinate needs a new skill, new knowledge or has a performance shortfall to correct. | Initiated by the subordinate; the subordinate seeks out the counsellor because of a problem (most often behavioural or attitudinal) where help in resolving it is needed. |
| Directive; the manager decides what to talk about and leads the subordinate in a pre-determined direction. | Non-directive; there is no pre-conceived idea about where the discussion will go. The counsellor follows the subordinate's lead. |
| Objective; the manager is impartial and focuses on the development of the subordinate. | Subjective; the counsellor must accept the subordinate's values and goals and be warm and non-judgemental. |

## DIFFERENCES BETWEEN COACHING AND MENTORING

Counselling is one of the 'softer' management skills, which has always been a part of effective managerial behaviour. Similarly, mentoring has always been with us, but is increasingly visible in management literature and in the practices of progressive companies as a major skill.

Mentoring has its origins in the concept of apprenticeship, when an older, more experienced individual passed down knowledge on how a task was done and how to operate in the commercial world. The mentor is interested in the career growth of capable younger protégés, and is willing to devote time and emotional energy to helping the young person (which would also provide the mentor with recognition and satisfaction). By contrast, coaching involves the subordinate in immediate improvement of performance, and the development of skills via a form of personal tutoring. Unlike coaching, mentoring is almost always concerned with the longer-term acquisition and application of skills in a developing career in the form of advising and counselling; coaching is more short term.

Biographies of gifted people repeatedly demonstrate the important contribution of the mentor in developing the individual. Andrew Carnegie, for example owed much to his senior, Thomas A Scott, who was head of the Western Division of the Pennsylvania Railroad. Scott recognized the talent of, and the desire to learn in, the young telegrapher and by providing him with the opportunity to learn through close personal observation, Scott added to Carnegie's self-confidence and sense of achievement. Because of his own personal strength and achievement, Scott did not fear Carnegie's aggressiveness; rather he gave it full play as a way of encouraging Carnegie's initiative.

Mentors take risks with people: they bet initially on talent they perceive in the young person and also risk emotional involvement in working closely with their juniors. These risks don't always pay off, but the willingness to take them appears crucial to developing future leaders. Of course, the range of skills that the manager as a coach needs in developing subordinates will also be appropriate for the mentor and vice versa (for example: good questioning techniques, goal setting, building rapport, giving and receiving feedback and constructive criticism). The mentor's role is more concerned with development than with actual training, but ultimately one leads to the other.

## DIFFERENCES BETWEEN COACHING AND TRAINING

Training, like coaching, as we have seen in Chapter 1, is a cost-effective way to increase productivity, reduce turnover, and keep the organization competitive in the market place and, like coaching, it frequently falls into the category of 'difficult to justify in times of recession', often being viewed as an overhead cost rather than as an investment. Coaching and training have other things in common. They both focus on the development of staff, and they both need implementing at the right time. Training options for employees are enormous, ranging from self-learning packages in all areas, through in-house and other training courses, to public seminars, conferences, and so on. However, each of these has potential drawbacks. For example, self-learning methods do not suit every-one because the element of human interaction – which is very important to some people – is missing; a great deal of self-motivation and perseverance is required to overcome feelings of isolation. Trainers and consultants obviously need to have a high level of competence and expertise if staff are to receive the right kind of training and to transfer that learning to their workplace. Public seminars and conferences allow employees to meet people from other organizations and departments for discussion, but are very costly to organize, and the content they offer for different levels, functions and types of organization can be too general in nature and not totally applicable to everyone's job.

At its best, training does offer many advantages to employees and organizations. It can improve attitudes, develop skills, impart new information and ideas, boost morale, help motivation and give increased incentive, especially if it can be transferred to other situations and become part of self-development. Coaching goes further than training, though, in that it is specific to organizational needs. Indeed, as Beggs (1992) has pointed out, new skills learnt in the classroom rarely carry over into the workplace successfully without the explicit support of the manager. It is clear that one of the most effective ways to develop the new skills is to use what is called 'follow-on coaching', which involves monitoring the effectiveness of what has been learnt as tasks are undertaken. Such coaching needs to be continued until the new skills are firmly established at a cost-effective level, and the manager is satisfied that learning has been effective – i.e. that the subordinate is using what has been learned to increase individual skill and improve not only working effectiveness but motivation and job satisfaction.

# LEARNING AND LEARNING STYLES

Training and learning are inextricably linked, but learning is such a fundamental process that many of us take it for granted. When asked to describe how they learned their jobs, most managers are likely to say they learned mostly from experience and practice (70 to 80 per cent according to Bass and Avolio, 1994). They acknowledge some formal training and other help, but stress that the responsibility which they have taken on and successful achievements in the job seem to account for most of their learning. However, it is uncertain whether subordinates will learn as effectively just from experience. Certainly managers who have been encouraged and helped to learn more effectively during their own careers will more readily appreciate the help and guidance a subordinate requires to succeed. While formal learning takes place through an inner drive (a natural subconscious process which responds to outer stimuli), informal learning just from experience can be an ill-defined, inefficient, hit-and-miss affair if there is no conscious effort to learn, or to demonstrate the knowledge and skills learnt through appropriate behaviours. The term 'learning style' is used to describe the attitudes and behaviours which determine an individual's preferred way of formal learning (Kolb, 1974). A person's learning style is the way in which that individual concentrates on, processes and retains new and difficult information, and engages in challenging tasks – an interaction process which is unique to each of us.

The manager as coach will highlight, from their own knowledge, skills, attitudes and experience, certain 'appropriate methods' which they think are particularly important and relevant to a particular task. However, the manager has to take into consideration the contribution the subordinate is able to make in terms of creative ideas, personal experiences, suggestions and preferred learning style. There are many influences on what is learned or not learned in the working environment. For example, past learning experiences may have been rewarding or demotivating, the methods of learning used adequate or inadequate, the blockages put on the learning – such as time constraints, place, and attitudes – inhibiting, and the perceived influences of boss, colleagues and associates, positive or negative.

The following six conditions need to be satisfied if effective learning is to take place:

- the **acceptance** that all subordinates can learn and are motivated to learn

- the attitude that **learning** is an active not a passive process

- that **guidance** is needed for the learner and can be provided by the use of learning methods which are both appropriate and varied

- that the learner should gain **satisfaction** from the learning process and **positive reinforcement** of the appropriate behaviour should be given

- that **short- and long-term goals** should specify attainable standards of performance

- the **recognition** that there are different levels of learning which take different times and which need different methods.

If the manager asks a subordinate to do something they have never done nor been taught before, expecting good performance the first time, that person will probably fail unless help and guidance are given. This is the widely used 'tell, leave alone and then criticize' approach some managers have to managing people. For example, if a manager, without analysing whether the subordinate can or is willing to do it, asks for a departmental budget to be prepared within ten days, the manager is likely to find all sorts of mistakes and problems in the finished piece of work if the subordinate is left to get on with it. The ensuing criticism is not likely to be viewed positively.

People develop individual preferences for certain behaviour patterns which can become habitual. One manager or subordinate may prefer to have a holistic view of the task to be achieved, while another may prefer to work step by step on each part in a sequential way until the overall picture emerges. Alternatively, one particular person may need to visualize ideas, while another may be happier discussing and describing the process verbally; yet another may prefer hands-on experience. Or again, one individual may jump to a certain course of action without giving adequate thought, analysis or review, when another may prefer long periods of deliberation. These 'styles' tend to be reinforced if a subordinate's style matches that of the manager, but if not, inadequate learning may result. If a manager is aware of their own and other's preferred learning styles, more effective learning is likely to take place within coaching sessions.

## THE FOUR LEARNING STYLES

Honey and Mumford (1992) have concluded from their experience and research that there are four main learning styles. These are:

**Activists** who involve themselves fully and without bias in new experiences, enjoy the here and now and are happy to be dominated by immediate experiences. They are open-minded and enthusiastic about anything new; they have a tendency to act first and consider the consequences afterwards and their days are filled with activity. They tackle problems by brainstorming, and as soon as the excitement from one activity has died down they are busy looking for the next. They tend to thrive on the challenge of new experiences but are bored with implementation and long-term consolidation. They are gregarious and are constantly involved with others but, in being so, they seek to centre all activities around themselves.

**Reflectors** like to stand back to ponder over and observe experiences from many different perspectives. They collect data about experiences and events, both first-hand and from others, and prefer to think about them thoroughly, postponing reaching definitive conclusions for as long as possible. Their philosophy is to be cautious, to consider all possible angles and implications before making a move. They prefer to take a back seat in meetings or discussions, and they enjoy observing other people in action. They listen to others and get the drift before making their own points. Overall, they tend to adopt a low profile and have a slightly distant, tolerant, unruffled air about them. When they act it is part of a wide picture which includes the past as well as the present, and others' observations as well as their own.

**Theorists** adapt and integrate observations into complex but logically sound theories. They think problems through in a vertical, step-by-step logical way. They assimilate disparate facts into coherent theories and tend to be perfectionists who will not rest until things are tidy and fit into a rational scheme. They like to analyse and synthesize, and are keen on basic assumptions, principles, theories, models and systems. Their philosophy prizes rationality and logic. They tend to be detached, analytical and dedicated to rational objectivity – to maximize certainty – rather than to anything subjective or ambiguous. Their approach to problems is consistently logical. This is their 'mental set'. and they rigidly reject anything that doesn't fit with it, feeling uncomfortable with subjective judgements, with lateral thinking, and with anything flippant.

**Pragmatists** are keen on trying out ideas, theories and techniques to see if they work in practice. They positively search out new ideas and take the first opportunity to experiment with applications. This is the type who returns from management courses brimming with new ideas that they want to practise; they like to get on with things, to act quickly and confidently on ideas that attract them. They tend to be impatient with open-ended questions as they are essentially practical, down-to-earth people who like making decisions and solving problems. They respond to problems and opportunities as a challenge.

Each style connects on a continuous learning cycle: having the experience (activist): reviewing the experience (reflector): concluding from the experience (theorist): and planning the next steps (pragmatist). If managers are aware of their own and others' learning style preferences, learning activities within the coaching sessions can be designed to encompass all learning styles.

STAGE 1
ACTIVIST
having an experience

STAGE 4
PRAGMATIST
planning the
next steps

STAGE 2
REFLECTOR
reviewing
the experience

STAGE 3
THEORIST
concluding from the experience

Cycle of Learning styles *From Honey and Mumford (1992)*

## WHAT IS YOUR PREFERRED LEARNING STYLE?

### EXERCISE 6

*When buying a new piece of domestic equipment (a new video recorder or dishwasher for instance), what do you prefer to do?*

(a) Take out the envelope that says 'read me first' and actually read it and the instruction book – perhaps even before taking the equipment out of its packaging, and certainly before trying to use it.

(b) Insist that the sales representative gives you a full demonstration and supervises you operating the process before you accept the equipment. As you install and operate it you will have the instruction book by your side.

(c) Forget all this. Just get your hands on it and play with it. You'll soon find out how it works. There's no time to mess around with over-complicated instruction books.

(d) There are a number of similarities between this equipment and its predecessor, which you identify. That makes life easier. You can now concentrate on the newer elements and will try to work out how they operate and then experiment with them. You will probably read the instruction book later to check your assumptions.

*Most likely you will prefer two of these and the other two will make you throw up your hands in horror!*

**(a) theorist**      **(b) reflector**
**(c) activist**      **(d) pragmatist**

The manager as coach should be aware of the influence these learning styles have on the way learning activities are approached, and on the way the task is structured for the individual. For example, for the **activist**, new experiences, challenges and problems, with opportunities to generate ideas will stimulate the learning process, but too much listening, observing of others, non-involvement and repetition will stifle the learning.

The **reflector** will learn best from activities where time is given to preparation and thinking, time to watch and listen and to mull over things, or to research and analyse before reading decisions and conclusions. This style dislikes role-playing, being asked to do something before having had the opportunity to plan, and having insufficient information at their disposal. Reflectors are worried by time pressures and deadlines – by any pressure to take shortcuts in the job.

The **theorist** will learn best from activities where a clear purpose is given together with time to explore the system or process. They prefer to make assessments and see the interrelationships between ideas as well as to question and work on complex problems. Theorists will learn least by being given activities that have no apparent purpose, method or structure. They will not learn well from demonstration without being given the theoretical basis as well, or from being asked to make quick decisions on shallow subjects. They can feel inhibited by other styles.

The **pragmatist** learns best from activities where techniques are shown by someone who has expertise in the subject and whom they might have a chance to emulate. There will be a wish to try things out and practise with lots of examples, and they will concentrate on the practical issues. This style will learn best from activities where the learning has practical benefit with little theory and general principles.

### Learning styles: action plans

Activist
> Give a variety of experiences and challenges. Support their enthusiasm but encourage them to plan ahead.

Reflector
> Give plenty of time to prepare, assimilate and consider alternatives.

Theorist
> Give many opportunities to question. Provide clear structure in goals and objectives at the beginning of the process together with complex ideas and concepts to work on. Allow time to review and reach conclusions.

Pragmatist
> Give plenty of opportunities to practise and offer tips and techniques. Offer the opportunity to plan future implementation.

To obtain the maximum benefit from the coaching process, the manager should ensure activities match the particular style or combination of styles of the subordinate. The manager will need to monitor and reflect on these activities with the subordinate as a result of the learning experiences gained. In addition to these individual subordinate learning styles, it is well to remember the manager's own learning style which probably influences their preferred coaching style, possibly without the manager being aware of it; an activist manager may well plunge the subordinate right into the middle of new experiences, believing in the 'sink or swim' concept and inviting sure failure if the subordinate is a reflector!

## IDENTIFYING SPECIFIC COACHING SKILLS AND ASSESSING THE SUBORDINATE

So far in this chapter we have stressed the importance of managerial functions such as planning and have looked at the role of learning styles. These come together in the manager's assessment of training needs, which is the first and probably the most important stage of the action plan. What skills, knowledge and characteristics are important to the particular task to be coached? This information is vital when considering the particular person to be coached and when establishing the specific task. Identifying the exact aspects of the task concerned and the qualities, characteristics, skills and competencies required for superior performance are all fundamental to the success of the coaching process. Such identification involves a detailed description of the particular job role, and should include a list of skills to be performed. The manager should also ask specific questions to ascertain the willingness and readiness of the person before the task is delegated.

The manager as coach will recognize that each individual's abilities and differences are the product of a unique combination of past history and experience. Everybody differs in what is brought to the job in terms of assumptions, capabilities and levels of interest, and in what can be contributed. In addition, each person is probably equally motivated and reinforced, or irritated and dissatisfied, by different things. Thus, the manager as a coach must have a recognition and acceptance of the concept of personal differences, make few assumptions, and have some idea of the differing strengths and weaknesses of each individual in order to understand how these may affect that person's functioning in the job. In addition, the manager should recognize that everyone's

## THE EXPERIENCE AND COMMITMENT OF THE SUBORDINATE

### EXERCISE 7

(a) What are the goals, objectives and responsibilities I want to develop and influence in this person?

..........................................................................................
..........................................................................................
..........................................................................................

(b) How much does he or she need to know and to change in order to be able to take on the responsibility for the task I want to delegate? To what extent do they have the necessary knowledge, skills, abilities and confidence?

..........................................................................................
..........................................................................................
..........................................................................................

(c) How well has this person performed in the past, and how are they performing at the present time?

..........................................................................................
..........................................................................................
..........................................................................................

(d) Is this individual ready and able to take on a new specific aspect of the job?

..........................................................................................
..........................................................................................
..........................................................................................

(e) How willing, enthusiastic, interested and motivated is the person to take on the responsibility for the task to be delegated?

..........................................................................................
..........................................................................................
..........................................................................................

contribution will be influenced by the manager's own characteristics and management style, as well as by the characteristics of the task itself. The performance and behaviour of each subordinate are the result of a complex interaction of the following separate qualities:

1. **Cognitive abilities** refer to someone's intellectual characteristics, which include the knowledge, skills and abilities that the person

develops and acquires through education or experience. These are the resources an individual brings to a task. Two classes of skills, knowledge and abilities are of particular importance to the coaching process – first, the general level of these attributes, and second, those relevant to the particular task (for example, organizational procedures and relevant technical knowledge). The successful manager as coach understands the task well enough to know what knowledge, skills and abilities are needed to bring a particular person up to standard. However, the manager may encounter instances where the most intelligent individual is not really contributing to task completion. This may happen when the person perceives the task as unimportant, or as lacking in challenge and stimulation. Research by Salancik and Pfeiffer (1978) has shown that the individual's *perception* of a task's merit is as important as more objective measures of its value.

2. **Personality characteristics** such as interest and values affect people's performance, motivation, commitment, involvement and loyalty. Research has shown that committed employees are more likely to accept the organization's goals and values, to experience positive or affective ties to colleagues, and to attempt to meet expectations (Steers, 1991). Greater commitment has also been shown to reduce absenteeism and staff turnover.

3. **Biographical and demographic characteristics** include such things as age, sex, race, health, marital status, geographic region of birth and upbringing, education level, and current and previous job experiences. The manager should recognize and identify key characteristics in these areas that can influence a person's perception of problems and acceptable solutions. For example, an older individual may view reorganization in a different way from someone who is younger.

## PARTICIPATION AND EFFECTIVENESS

The criteria for a subordinate's performance should be mutually decided in advance of the coaching sessions. In making this decision, both manager and subordinate should consider both short- and long-term goals, first because they will be instrumental in determining the basis on which effort will be judged and, second, because such consideration involves the subordinate in the planning process, which increases commitment to the goals and objectives established. In setting these short- and long-term goals it is important that they are programmed so that they are stretching but achievable, so that the person proceeds along the path of gradual and systematic development, and will reach the point of good performance. The manager needs to devote time to nurture a positive climate, motivation, morale and commitment to objectives, as well as decision-making, communication and problem-solving skills through the coaching process. These enable the individual to assume more and more responsibility for personal performance and to be confident enough to express ideas and feelings. Likert (1961) found that subordinates generally responded well to high expectations and to a manager's genuine confidence in them and, in turn, tried to justify those expectations. The resulting high performance reinforces the manager's trust in the subordinate. Livingston (1969) in discussing this phenomenon, refers to the words of Eliza Dolittle in the play *Pygmalion*:

> You see, really and truly, apart from the things anyone can pick up (the dressing and the proper way of speaking, and so on), the difference between a lady and a flower girl is not how she behaves but how she's treated. I shall always be a flower girl to Professor Higgins, because he always treats me as a flower girl, and always will; but I know I can be a lady to you, because you always treat me as a lady, and always will.

Livingston found that some managers always treat their subordinates in a way that leads to superior performance. If a manager's expectations were high, productivity was likely to be excellent: if expectations were low, productivity was poor. When the subordinate responds to the manager's high expectations with high performance, Livingston referred to it as the 'effective cycle'.

The role the manager plays in the coaching process in developing the readiness of the subordinate is very important. Initially the manager takes an active role by providing structure, direction and close supervision – especially when working with people who have little experience of the task or the workings of the department. As each person's performance improves, so more responsibility and opportunities for achievement, development and growth can be given.

# TASK DEMANDS

Once the goals, objectives and responsibilities are identified and understood for a given task, the manager must specify clearly what constitutes good performance in each area, so that both manager and subordinate know when performance has reached the desired level. If the person is able to do some part of the task without direction but feels insecure then the manager is faced with a motivational problem. In such a case the manager should be very supportive and build on what the person is already capable of doing. For example, if the manager wants someone to take on the responsibility of developing a departmental budget:

1. The manager would need to initiate the task by telling the person exactly what would be involved in developing this budget (for example, present costs as compared with last year's, and so on).

2. The manager would explain how, what, when and where to do each of the tasks involved, and begin to focus on performance. (Learning style would also be taken into consideration at this point).

3. The manager would then take a small risk and begin to delegate some part of the responsibility for one of the tasks within the assignment by reducing the amount of direction and supervision given, thus gearing the person for success, and hopefully ensuring that the quality of the work will be high.

4. The manager would create a learning environment in which the person feels confident in taking responsibility for the task progressively – i.e. immediately rewarding progress and adequate performance, thus giving positive strokes (verbally and non-verbally) and increasing the likelihood of recurring success and overall competence.

5. The manager would continue this process until the person comes close to the expected performance for the whole task, and then remain on hand to provide a moderate amount of support when needed. How much time will be needed overall for coaching sessions will vary, and will depend on the individual and the difficulty of the task.

It is important that the manager does not delegate too much responsibility too soon otherwise this may set the person up for failure or deter them from taking on responsibility in the future. There can be a danger also in giving too much praise and positive reinforcement if progress has not been made towards the desired result. If the manager finds the subordinate unable to cope with the assigned responsibility, a repetition of the instructions should be given or more direction supplied. The manager would do well to remember that as someone changes, his or her motives and position in the needs hierarchy will often change too. For example, once the subordinate is confident in the job, less socio-emotional support will be needed. This concept of positive reinforcement of successive behaviour is associated with the behaviour modification and reinforcement theory of Skinner (1953) and with performance management theory (Bandura, 1969). Skinner's theory is explained more fully in Chapter 4 under *Positive Supportive Feedback*.

## SUCCESSFUL COACHING

Successful coaching, as we have seen, brings benefit to the manager, to the subordinate and to the organization. These benefits include improvement in work quality and in motivation and a heightened perception of roles by everyone. This, of course, can lead to recognition and reward as well as improved relationships within the department.

Successful coaching processes, since they are based on a one-to-one, interactive dialogue, demand a high level of communication skills – skills which are reviewed in the next chapter. The process also demands a high level of discipline in that coaching focuses on actual problems or opportunities; that is, things which can be improved or changed in someone's performance or in the department's operation. These elements must be capable of objective description so that it is possible to aim for clear goals and objectives to improve productivity and efficiency. Coaching is an organized and disciplined process which nonetheless aims, in addition to more quantifiable results, at mutual exploration, discovery and continual learning.

During the coaching process the subordinate is facing new challenges and taking responsibility for learning and for goal setting in the new situation. In the relatively sheltered environment of the coaching process (sheltered in that the manager is on hand to minimize external threats to learning), new and creative ideas as well as new insights broaden the perspective of the person being coached, and, hopefully, stimulate their curiosity. This in turn generates further change in commitment, awareness, attitudes and behaviour, as well as developing adaptability and flexibility. There are certain 'givens' in the change process:

- **From dependence to autonomy.** This is allowing, encouraging and possibly at times forcing someone to make decisions and think things out – even if it takes longer and even if the manager may disagree with their decisions. The manager needs to offer support for the person's ideas and should give them a fair chance, even if they are unusual. The whole process is hindered if the manager imposes solutions, tries to take short cuts, or tries to prove that ideas they disagree with will not work.

- **From ignorance to insight.** Here the subordinate is encouraged to think out reasons, to make tentative generalizations and to draw parallels with what might have already happened in the past.

- **From selfishness to altruism.** The subordinate needs to be rewarded for personal success but should also be rewarded for things that impact on others (such as considering the implications of plans or ideas on others' feelings – involving or consulting with the other people affected by them). This process will be hindered if only individual effort and achievement is given praise and its contribution to overall group or organizational success remains unacknowledged.

- **From a need for certainty to a tolerance for ambiguity.** The manager should encourage consideration of alternative courses of action and should support the subordinate in risk-taking or in trying out ideas, even when outcomes are uncertain. If the manager allows the person to adopt the first solution that comes along instead of insisting on looking at alternatives and their implications, then both learning and the process of change are considerably impeded.

- **From the routine to the more complex.** The manager needs to allow the individual to tackle problems which require new skills and experience, calling for levels of knowledge which move from the relatively shallow to relatively deep abilities. This involves tension for the person partly because of the newness of the situation and partly because of fear of failure so that active encouragement and support from the manager is critically important for long-term success.

- **From negative to positive self-image.** The manager can support this change by giving praise for strengths displayed and by offering non-evaluative, factual feedback on areas for improvement. Where the latter is necessary, the manager must focus on behaviour, not personality, and should encourage exploration for improvement without in any way belittling someone's efforts or emphasizing weaknesses in ideas.

## Characteristics of successful coaches

Good coaches:

- are interested in the individual's development
- look for potential in the person
- help the individual to think independently
- are predictable and straightforward
- let the person know where they stand
- give due credit to the person
- build and show confidence
- take risks to help the person learn
- have high standards that are communicated
- are good facilitators of learning
- encourage the person to want to give of their best
- never miss an opportunity to coach.

Managers should be committed to the coaching of subordinates as part of their job description, and should see their role as helping others to grow professionally, to take on increased responsibility for more tasks, and to develop their potential for quality performance in the job. This chapter has looked at the meaning of coaching; Chapter 4 considers the factors involved in the coaching programme itself.

To summarize:

❏ A structured plan of action is needed for coaching to ensure that the manager really encourages learning.

❏ Factors to consider include the standard managerial functions of planning, organizing, motivating and influencing.

❏ A coach may have to change their pattern of behaviour towards others, and the 'unfreezing' which is needed before learning takes place can be unsettling, even threatening.

❏ Coaching differs in many respects from counselling and from mentoring, although these last two skills are also critical. While being close to training, coaching also differs from it in many ways, although 'follow-on' coaching can be used after training to ensure the implementation of new skills or approaches to tasks.

❏ Six conditions need to be satisfied for effective learning. If they are disregarded, failure becomes more likely.

❏ We all have favoured learning styles. One model suggests that there are four main learning approaches – activist, reflector, theorist and pragmatist.

❏ It is important to understand the needs of each of the four approaches to ensure that learning takes place. The coaching approach of the manager may be affected unwittingly by their own preferred style.

❏ A first stage of any action plan is an assessment of the subordinate to determine their experience and commitment.

❏ The subordinate brings to the task a unique set of cognitive abilities, personality characteristics and biographical and demographic attributes.

❏ Criteria for evaluating good performance must be clearly established beforehand. Time also needs to be given to creating the right climate and to developing the readiness of the person.

❏ Too much delegation too quickly can cause problems in the future, as can giving praise without positive performance to justify it.

❏ Successful coaching brings benefits to all concerned in the process. There are, however, performance criteria which need to be satisfied for the benefits to be realized.

❏ There are also six change criteria such as the move from dependence to autonomy which are 'givens' if coaching is to bring about significant behaviour change.

❏ Successful coaches share some common characteristics.

# Chapter Four

# How Is Coaching Done?

With the influence of down-sizing, restructuring and increased specialization within organizations, managers have been forced to rethink how they manage. They need to be able to share greater work-loads with staff and continuously to develop the human resources at their disposal to higher levels of potential and commitment. Managers who like to make all the decisions, and subordinates who happily give up this responsibility, get caught in an unproductive cycle; the staff don't learn to make decisions, while managers don't learn to delegate and the organization as a whole suffers.

## WHICH BEHAVIOURS CAN AND CAN'T BE COACHED?

As shown earlier, coaching means different things to different people. Coaching is a one-to-one activity, usually conducted on the job, with the objective of improving the willingness and ability of the person to perform a specific task which is assigned by the manager, who then gives encouragement and support. There are as many different applications for coaching skills as there are training needs. Some of these are:

- When the subordinate is new to a job or project; for example, a young manager or supervisor who is promoted to head a team.

- When the subordinate can learn from another's success; for example, when a key project has just been successful.

- When the subordinate can learn from an unsuccessful project or from targets not having been met; when mistakes have been made and lessons can be learned from them.

- When the subordinate has a specific difficulty with a piece of work or a problem to solve; for example, in needing a new perspective or a creative solution.

Anyone who has the expertise to transfer skills and experience in a relevant on-the-job setting can coach. Here, we are considering the relationship between the manager and the subordinate in the coaching situation. The forging of this relationship can help break down restrictive and limiting hierarchies and create that climate of open communication discussed earlier. Coaching can help in furthering the development of both parties, can give job satisfaction, increase motivation and nurture management potential. There are, of course, some things that belong solely to the manager's job that should not be coached: for example, responsibilities that demand his or her specific attention, such as handling a staff member's personal problem, or duties inherent in the job such as achieving organizational goals. Again, the manager cannot coach for attitude change; he or she can only hold up the mirror and let the subordinate take the initiative.

## SELF-CONCEPT

The way the mirror is held up, or the things the mirror has chosen to reflect can have a large bearing on an individual's self-concept. Individuals learn who they are from the way they are treated by the important people in their lives, by significant others. From the verbal and non-verbal communication with these significant others, individuals learn whether others like or dislike, accept or reject them, whether they are worthy of respect or disdain, or are a success or a failure. If those individuals are to have a strong self-concept, they need love, respect and acceptance from these others in their lives. Self-concept of both manager and subordinate are critical factors in effective communication in the coaching situation. While this situation may change from moment to moment or from place to place, people's beliefs about themselves are always determining factors within it. The self is the star in every act of communication and the self-concept is the centre of a person's universe – a frame of reference for their personal reality. It is a special vantage point – a screen through which everything else is seen, heard, evaluated and understood: it is a filter of the world around. Linked to self-concept is the belief that the person has rights, such as the right to change one's mind, the right to say 'I don't understand', 'I don't know' or 'I'm not sure, but let me work on it'. Believing in such rights can help strengthen the manager's and the subordinate's self-concept and avoid the defensive behaviours that hinder communication and the exchange of information.

Good self-concepts are thus critical factors in the ability of both manager and staff member to be effective communicators, in the experiencing of a healthy and satisfying interaction in the coaching situation. If the subordinate has a weak self-concept, this will often distort beliefs about what the manager thinks; it may generate feelings of insecurity and cause difficulty in conversing or expressing ideas and feelings about work – even about whether to give or accept constructive criticism. These problems will result in further feelings of inadequacy and inferiority, in diminished confidence, and in the rejection of one's own ideas as lacking interest and being unworthy of expression. If, on the other hand, both manager and subordinate communicate effectively one to the other, thoughts, feelings and needs are made known. It is appropriate at this point to look at communication in more detail.

## COMMUNICATION SKILLS INVOLVED IN THE COACHING PROCESS

Successful coaching involves many communication and behavioural skills. These will be considered throughout this chapter under specific headings.

### EFFECTIVE COMMUNICATION

Communication is a cycle or loop that involves at least two people. When people are communicating, they perceive and filter their responses, and react with their own thoughts and feelings. Their on-going behaviour is generated by their internal responses to what they see, hear and feel. It is the attention that each pays to the other verbally and non-verbally that gives them ideas about what to say or do next. For example, tone of voice and body language determine whether the word 'Hello' is a simple recognition, a threat, a put-down, or a delightful greeting. To be an effective communicator, the manager should act on the principle that 'The meaning of the communication is the response you get' (O'Connor and Seymour, 1990). When people communicate they use skills to influence other people, but at the same time they should respect and appreciate that others have different maps of the world and may see, hear and feel things differently.

Good communication is at the heart of the coaching process, which aims at a mutual consultation and agreement between manager and subordinate, as has been pointed out. For success, the lines of communication need to be wide open. The general climate during coaching should be congenial in order to increase rapport and the receptivity of the subordinate. Accordingly, it is important for the manager to remember that communication is greatly enhanced by how the problems and issues to be discussed and worked on are perceived by both parties. For example, the subordinate must know not only the specific performance expected, but also precisely how attainment of the goals will be evaluated. Communication can become distorted if mutual empathy is not established, and if both points of view are not taken into consideration. In addition, non-verbal communication, (i.e. gestures, posture, tone of voice, expressions) is possibly as important as verbal communication. Research leads to the conclusion that there is a positive correlation between effective communication and each of the following factors in the work place: subordinate productivity, personal satisfaction, rewarding relationships and effective problem-solving (Luthi, 1978).

In order to become effective communicators, the manager and the subordinate need to listen not only to the words spoken, but to the way these words are expressed, and to the non-verbal signs which convey and demonstrate interest, attention, understanding and concern for needs and problems. This effective communication is also dependent on the following forms.

The **words and phrases** selected: words can insult, injure and exalt, can lead to costly errors, false hopes and disillusionment. They can also invoke pride, loyalty, action and silence. Whatever they provoke, they are critical in the effectiveness of the communication process.

The secret of good communication is not so much what is said, but how it is said. The ability of the voice to affect how something is said is known as **paralanguage**. Its characteristics are rate of speech, diction, tone, rhythm and volume. These can convey enthusiasm, anxiety, confidence, urgency, serenity and other states of mind and intentions. The timing of the words spoken, the intensity of the voice, the pauses and the variations in pitch can all increase the ability of the speaker to influence. By closely attending to a person's paralanguage, the manager as coach can pick up all sorts of clues as to how the process is progressing.

**Non-verbal behaviour** includes anything that can be seen by the other person, such as eye contact, positioning, body language, facial expressions and gestures.

How the manager approaches the coaching session, how the messages conveyed are supported or not by gestures and facial expressions, how interest and attention are influenced through eye contact and other non-verbal behaviour, will all affect the way in which the subordinate reacts. In addition, the subordinate's non-verbal cues will give the manager insight into how the messages have been received. For example, movement towards the front of the chair may indicate interest, but could also mean the subordinate is wanting to get away from the situation (the quality of eye contact and perhaps the position of the feet will give clues as to which it is). If the subordinate mirrors the manager's gestures and position, this may well indicate agreement and acceptance. It is appropriate at this point to look at some of these aspects of communication in more detail.

## CONDITIONS WHICH HINDER EFFECTIVE COMMUNICATION

In simple terms, communication can be considered as the sending and receiving of messages, since both elements must be present for it to take place. However, the fact that a message has been sent and received does not mean that total communication has occurred. Often it may have been only partial, or have been distorted as a result of the context in which it takes place. This context may be environmental, emotional, physical, or may arise from a host of conditions present within the individuals attempting to communicate. When the manager is communicating with the subordinate in the coaching process, the messages pass through 'perceptual filters', and because of these filters, there is the potential for communication to break down at any part in the process. For example, the manager's and the subordinate's perceptions can be affected by different dimensions of the messages transmitted and received, i.e. the words used, the non-verbals and the paralanguage. In the coaching process the key to success is an awareness of all the conditions which can interfere with effective communication.

## Conditions blocking or altering the intention of messages

- **Preoccupation:** an individual who is focusing on internal stimuli may listen in such a way that little or none of the message comes through.

- **Emotion:** words may have become emotion-charged, due to early conditioning or to circumstances in the individual's life at the time of communicating.

- **Hostility:** anger may be generated during the communication, or may be carried over from a recent experience. The subject matter itself may arouse hostility, and this may distort the message being communicated, causing further hostility.

- **Charisma:** an individual who has something important to contribute yet who lacks charisma may not be able to hold attention in order to convey the message he or she wants to communicate. Also, if a person is charismatic, it can embarrass or make the other person feel ill at ease or cause them feelings of inferiority.

- **Past experiences:** these can predispose receivers of information not to listen. On the other hand, an individual with a special interest (that is, a hidden agenda) may hear all messages only in reference to their personal needs, or may reject or manipulate messages which do not relate to their own interests.

- **Inarticulateness:** lack of verbal skill may distort the intention of the sender of the message. If the receiver of the message is unaware of the sender's difficulty or of cultural differences, again the message may be dismissed or misinterpreted.

- **Stereotyping:** the visual impact of the speaker may change the perception of the communication. A very conventional individual may 'hear' all attempts at communication as radical if the speaker has a non-conventional physical appearance.

- **Physical environment:** physical surroundings can create conditions under which effective communication cannot take place. An individual's physical state may also be detrimental to effective communication (for example, physical needs causing the mind to wander or withdraw).

- **Defensiveness:** insecurity within an individual tends to distort questions into accusations, and replies into justifications.

- **Relationship and status:** two sets of messages may be given out simultaneously when attempting to communicate – content and relationship. A person may be so preoccupied with listening for any cues to the latter that the former is lost or seriously distorted. Furthermore, a person may find it difficult to communicate with people who are in a position of higher status because of their perceived (or enforced) power or aggressiveness.

## DEFENSIVE COMMUNICATION

Other ways of communicating effectively include speaking clearly, maintaining an attentive posture, being honest and timely, listening actively, and paraphrasing for emphasis and attention. These principles are important to the manager as coach in improving their skills of expression and listening, but the climate in which the communication takes place is even more important. A supportive climate promotes understanding and problem-solving, while a defensive one impedes them.

Let's take the second point first. A principal motive behind defensive communication is control. Although control can take different forms, it is often shown by communication which is designed to persuade. The manager may be friendly, patient, and courteous, but their goal is to convince other people that as manager, they are in control. As this interaction continues, both manager and subordinate become less able to 'hear' each other or to perceive accurately one another's motives, values and emotions. In short, communication breaks down. For example, if a subordinate continues to question the validity of the manager's request, one or both of them will inwardly or outwardly become critical of the other. Their dialogue may appear calm and friendly but their feelings will become obvious. The longer this conversation continues, the more frustration ensues until each begins to see the other as stubborn, unreasonable and possibly stupid. Regardless of the outcome, feelings for each other are likely to be negative, and commitment to following through on agreed action will be low. Obviously the effect of this, especially if the situation if repeated, is poor in the long-term as well as the short-term. There is another way, however!

## SUPPORTIVE COMMUNICATION

A supportive climate is built on understanding. It also involves risk, but risks will need to be taken in the coaching situation if thoughts and feelings are to be shared genuinely. Supportive communication involves a shift from thinking in terms of pre-conceived answers to thinking in terms of the goals a subordinate needs to accomplish, and then co-operating to seek solutions within the coaching process to satisfy those needs. Coach and subordinate establish a dialogue, listen to each other, and appreciate and explore differences of opinion. The characteristic results of good communication are:

- **Empathy** or 'catching each other's feelings' – i.e. showing respect for one another's thoughts or views.

- **Spontaneity** – being open, uninhibited, responsive, and feeling free to express thoughts and feelings.

- **Problem-solving** – willingness to explore differences, share perceptions, tolerate one another's perspectives and resolve conflict in a mutually satisfying way.

- **Synergy** – outcomes that combine elements of contrasting positions into a new and meaningful solution that satisfies the needs of both coach and subordinate – a win-win situation.

In coaching it is vital that both manager and subordinate have an awareness of the other's feelings, and vital that they stop and check these from time to time. Each may feel a range of emotions, so it is essential that behaviours are identified and the feelings that are causing those behaviours dealt with. The communication process is complex, but vital if coach and subordinate are to achieve sufficient clarity to handle each situation adequately.


## METACOMMUNICATION

We communicate with others on two levels – denotative and metacommunicative: the former deals with the words we say, the straightforward verbal content of the message: the latter refers to the way we communicate *about* our communication. For example, the tone of voice used by a manager to say, 'Get out of my office' tells the other person how to interpret the words – whether serious or not. The metacommunicative aspects of the voice indicate a request that interprets the verbal, denotative message in certain ways. We use metacommunication largely to make requests of the person with whom we are interacting. It can be explicit and verbal or can consist of less obvious, non-verbal cues. By interpreting messages on both levels – denotative and metacommunicative – the subordinate decides what the manager means and acts on that basis. Because so many metacommunications are non-verbal, conflicting messages can emerge: 'What does the manager really mean?'. If the manager as coach is more aware of how they are communicating and metacommunicating, they can ensure that requests made to others will be successful.

---

## COMMUNICATION: QUESTIONS FOR MANAGERS TO BEAR IN MIND

### EXERCISE 8

• Am I aware of the messages of my non-verbal behaviour and my tone of voice?

..........................................................................
..........................................................................
..........................................................................

• What conclusions can I draw about my staff from their verbal and non-verbal communication?

..........................................................................
..........................................................................
..........................................................................

• What changes would I like to make in my communication with my staff – verbally, tone of voice or non-verbally?

..........................................................................
..........................................................................
..........................................................................

• How might I accomplish these changes? What obstacles might stand in my way?

..........................................................................
..........................................................................
..........................................................................

• What might the benefits be if I change my communication behaviour with my staff – verbally, tone of voice, non-verbally etc?

..........................................................................
..........................................................................
..........................................................................

## ACTIVE LISTENING

One way of checking that manager and subordinate are clear about emotions and about the other's view of the situation is to listen actively rather than passively. Many people find it difficult to say what they mean or to express what they feel. They often assume that others understand what they mean, even if they are careless or unclear in their speech, and it is this assumption that forms one of the most difficult barriers to successful communication. Some poor listening habits include:

- **Inattention** – for instance thinking of other things, playing with papers on the desk or interrupting the session by answering telephone calls.

- **Pretending to listen** – thus leaving the speaker with a wrong impression of what has been achieved.

- **Listening until there is something to say** – then stopping listening and starting to rehearse what to say, and preparing to interrupt at the earliest possible opportunity.

- **Hearing what is expected** – thinking what has been heard is what was expected, or refusing to hear what one does not want to hear.

- **Feeling defensive** – assuming that the speaker's intention is known and, for various reasons, expecting to be attacked by what is said.

- **Listening for points of disagreement** – waiting for the chance to attack by listening intently for points of disagreement instead of concentrating on the positives.

Essential prerequisites for improving listening skills are being aware of one's own listening behaviour and having the motivation to improve it. Such improvement demands that we adopt what is called *active listening* which is defined as a communication skill to help people solve their own problems. It is not intended to be manipulative or to make people behave or think in ways that others think they should. To be effective, the listener should take an 'active' responsibility to understand the content and feeling of what is being said. The listener can respond with a statement, in their own words, of what they feel the sender's message means. For example:

**Sender:** 'The deadline for this assignment is totally unrealistic!'

**Listener:** 'You feel you will find it stressful to get the assignment done on time.'

This can then lead to appropriate actions to deal with the real concerns.

Much communication training focuses on skills of self-expression and persuasion, with little attention paid to listening to the complete message that the other person is communicating. Yet it is the element of feeling which gives the message its real meaning. Active listening integrates physical, emotional and intellectual inputs in the search for meaning and understanding. Reik (1972) refers to the process of active listening as 'listening with the third ear'. A listener's third ear, as Reik describes, hears what is said between sentences and without words, what is expressed soundlessly, what the speaker feels and thinks. As expression of emotions is vital to building a good relationship between manager and subordinate, both need to express their feelings constructively rather than destructively. Clearly then, listening should not be a passive process, but an integral and active part of good communication.

An open communication climate is essential if better understanding is to be achieved. The manager and the subordinate can further help to create this climate if they:

- **Put themselves in each other's place** – have a reason or purpose for listening, and feed back their perceptions of the intended meaning to check for accuracy of listening and understanding.

- **Listen for the whole message** – look for meaning and consistency or congruence in both the verbal and non-verbal messages received; listen for ideas, feelings and intentions as well as facts and hear things that are sometimes unpleasant or unwelcome – not only positive things.

- **Suspend judgement** – and listen without drawing premature conclusions.

- **Resist distractions** – (noises, views, people) and focus on the speaker.

- **Wait before responding** – too prompt a response reduces listening effectiveness and allows no time to assimilate the information.

- **Paraphrase** the content and feeling of what has been said non-judgementally to the satisfaction of the other, and use open questions to discover exactly what was meant, thus avoiding misunderstandings and misinterpretations.

- **Seek the important themes** of what is being said by listening for the real meaning contained in the spoken words.

- **Use the time differential** between the rate of speech and the rate of thought to reflect on the content and meaning and to give time to process the information.

- **Be ready to respond** to ideas, suggestions and comments in a non-accusing manner rather than giving advice or making judgements.

A subordinate needs to know that the manager is listening actively and paying attention to what he or she says. The manager can demonstrate this by assuming and maintaining an attentive posture (for instance, maintaining eye contact, nodding, making encouraging noises), by paraphrasing, by mirroring body movements and by reflecting on what was said to ensure that the message has been understood as intended. For example, if a subordinate says, 'I'm really annoyed. I've been conscientious, worked very hard, but still I haven't been promoted', the manager might begin their response by paraphrasing: 'You feel that you haven't been recognized for your efforts', thus demonstrating that the message has been heard and understood.

## NEURO-LINGUISTIC PROGRAMMING (NLP)

An increasingly popular approach to communication, which goes even beyond the concepts of active listening and the other aspects of metacommunication described, is based on 'Neuro-linguistic programming'. This is an explicit and powerful model of human experience and communication. **Neuro** refers to the nervous system (the mind) through which our experience is processed via five senses: visual, auditory, kinesthetic, olfactory and gustatory. **Linguistic** refers to language and other non-verbal communication systems through which our neural representations are coded, ordered and given meaning. These include pictures, sounds, feelings, tastes, smells and words (internal dialogue). **Programming** refers to the ability to discover and utilize the programmes that we run (our communication to ourselves and others) in our neurological systems to achieve our specific and desired outcomes.

# CORRECTING POOR LISTENING HABITS

### EXERCISE 9

*Which of the following apply to you?*

1. INATTENTION
   Recognize the need to listen without thinking of other things, playing with papers on the desk or allowing telephone calls to interrupt.

2. PRETENDING TO LISTEN
   Concentrate on listening to what is being said and show you are listening actively by interacting with the person and providing them with verbal and non-verbal proof that you understand.

3. LISTENING UNTIL YOU HAVE SOMETHING TO SAY
   Search for the meaning in the communication instead of focusing on what you wish to contribute, change or are annoyed about. Avoid the temptation to interrupt at the earliest possible opportunity.

4. HEARING WHAT IS EXPECTED
   Search for the meaning in the communication rather than focus on what you expect to hear. Do not anticipate what the person will say or complete statements for them.

5. FEELING DEFENSIVE
   Listen patiently to the person's fears and problems as well as their accomplishments. Do not automatically guess their intentions. Do not expect to be attacked.

6. RESPONDING EMOTIONALLY
   Repress the tendency to respond emotionally to what is said or what you think has been said. Think about why the person said what they did and how you can respond constructively.

This began in the 1970s in the USA when John Grinder, a professor of linguistics, and Richard Bandler, a mathematician, studied three celebrated therapists, all of whom had achieved excellence in their work. The aim of the study was to determine the common characteristics that contributed to personal excellence. In particular, Grinder and Bandler contrasted these expert communicators with average communicators to discover if there were hidden skills that could account for the differences. Their findings suggested that there were indeed key differences and that these variables lay in thinking strategies, unconscious beliefs, and in verbal and non-verbal behaviour. Neuro-linguistic programming is the current practice which describes these variables in more precise detail. Since a person's external behaviour provides clues to their internal processing, the most useful NLP concepts for the manager as coach are:

- **Calibration:** recognizing when a person is in a different mental state. This is a skill the manager possesses and uses every day in his working environment: for example, having the experience of talking to a colleague or member of staff and getting an intuition that things are not quite right. The manager calibrates this unconsciously, and feels this without knowing why. However, using this awareness to reach hasty conclusions about the meaning of the behaviour observed is a trap one can easily fall into. It is all too easy to make hasty judgements that a person is miserable, anxious or defensive. This sort of labelling is usually an unconscious reaction based on past experience in our own personal history and it may be incorrect to apply that judgement to that particular person. There is room for this type of judgement, but it is within the context of careful observation and listening. In NLP, eye position, angle of the head, breathing (whether deep or shallow, fast or slow), changes in lip size and shape, and tone of voice are all important. These subtle signs are outward expressions of inner thoughts and are normally disregarded. However, since people's behaviour is remarkably consistent, it is possible to recognize different 'states' in an individual and to rely on that observation. The process of calibrating for the manager as coach breaks down into three steps: **look and listen** to notice consistent patterns of behaviour especially when asking questions and actively listening for the answers; **pause**, and **check out** your intuition before reaching a **conclusion** about what the behaviour means.

- **Rapport:** if the meaning of the communication resides in the response it elicits, gaining rapport is the ability to elicit desired outcomes. The ability to get on with other people, to interact and to maintain rapport whether in teams, gathering information, in negotiations with customers, or dealing with the people above or below us, is one of the keys to success in the working environment.This rapport does or does not develop naturally – there are some people we get on with at once, some we grow to like, and some with whom we are never comfortable, however long we know them. NLP provides the manager (and the subordinate) with skills they can use when they need to generate good working relationships, especially in the coaching process. We have all had experiences of what is said to us verbally or shown non-verbally creating or destroying our communication with the other person. People who are in rapport, however, tend unconsciously to mirror and match each other in posture, gesture, eye contact, and even their language seems to be complementary.

One way to increase rapport for the manager as coach is to increase rapport by deliberately matching, with respect, care and subtlety, the body language and postures of the person they are communicating with: for example, matching overall sitting or standing posture, crossing or uncrossing of limbs, breathing, facial expressions, gestures. Also, matching breathing, by observing or working out their rhythm from the rhythm of their talking, can be a very powerful way of generating rapport. Another powerful way for the manager to gain rapport with the subordinate he or she is coaching is to match their voice, voice patterns and the words they use: for example, matching volume, tone, timbre (quality) and tempo of the voice as well as the key words and length of phrases and sentences they use. For example, we use words to describe our thoughts, therefore our choice of words will indicate how we are thinking. Consider three people who have just read the same report. The first might say that he *saw* a lot in it, the examples were well chosen to *illustrate* the subject and it was written in a *bubbling* style. The second might object to the *tone* of the report, and he was unable to *tune in* to the writer's ideas at all, and would like to *tell* him so. The third *feels* the report dealt with a *weighty* subject in a *balanced* way and liked the way the writer *touched on* all the key points. They all read the same report but how they thought about it they expressed in different ways: one was thinking in *pictures*, the second in *sounds* and the third in *feelings*. It is possible for the manager as coach to find out a person's preferred style by heightening sensory acuity in noticing, hearing and picking up the other person's language patterns and responding in the same representational system, i.e.

letting the visualizers see what is being said: the auditory thinkers hear what is being said and getting the kinesthetic thinkers to grasp the meaning of what is being said.

- **Pacing and leading:** the process of building better communication is seen to depend upon the development of these two concepts. *Pacing* is establishing a bridge through rapport and respect. For example, when the person being coached is anxious, appropriate mirroring of posture, the matching of normal breathing and voice tonality, tempo, pitch and volume, are all effective ways of building rapport and harmonizing with how that person feels. This can then be followed by gradual changes and adjustment to a more positive and resourceful posture. If the bridge is successfully built, the other person will then follow the lead. They will perceive unconsciously that their state is respected and be willing to follow. *Leading* follows on directly from pacing. As rapport is established, a link is felt and a point is reached where change is initiated which goes beyond just mirroring, when the other person will unconsciously follow. Pacing and leading are powerful tools for building rapport. At their best, they incorporate the matching of small arm or hand movements, body and head movements (called *cross-over mirroring*) and basic posture: they take care to avoid mimicry, which is the noticeable, exaggerated and indiscriminate copying of another's movements, a practice which can be considered offensive. Pacing and leading involves matching the person for a while until a level of rapport is reached that the manager is happy with. If then the manager starts to closely change what is being done, the person being coached will follow if there is good rapport. In this way, the manager can lead the subordinate into adopting a different position on the problem being discussed.

Once the simple techniques of NLP are learnt, they can go some way to helping the manager (and the subordinate) recognize signs of doubt and misunderstanding in themselves and the person with whom they are communicating, and can deal promptly to increase the chances of the communication being successful.

## QUESTIONING

Listening is a vital and active skill, as we have seen. Complementary to listening is the pro-active skill of questioning. This is one of the basic and most important skills the manager as coach needs to perfect. The questions asked should be positive and stretching, and should encourage the subordinate to think through the implications of ideas, suggestions, and the like. During a coaching session, the manager will ask questions for the purposes of obtaining information, establishing rapport and clarifying or stimulating thinking and creativity, respectively. Pareek and Rao (1990) have suggested that certain types of questions should be avoided in the coaching situation. These are summarized as follows:

- **Critical and sarcastic questions** that are used to reprimand or to express doubt about someone's abilities, and which create a gap between the manager and subordinate. For example, when discussing performance standards which may not have been met, the manager should be aware of the type of phrases used. 'Why did you fail to meet the deadline for the last task?' communicates criticism, whereas, 'What might account for the lateness in meeting the last deadline?' invites examination of the reasons and a discussion of possible procedures to avoid such lateness in the future. Critical questions undermine confidence and may lead to resentment, hostility and the suppression of ideas and motivation.

- **Testing questions** designed to determine whether the person is 'right' or 'wrong' and to discover how much they know. Such questions can imply a superior attitude of cross-examination on the part of the manager.

- **Leading questions** that may elicit a false answer from the subordinate. For example, 'Were you unable to meet your last deadline because of other problems in the department?' This type of question can seduce the person into giving a reply that the manager wants to hear, and can put a stop to further exploration of the issue.

## OPEN AND CLOSED QUESTIONS

The types of question asked, the manner in which they are asked and the language used (remembering what was said earlier about matching voice and the key words and phrases), can either facilitate or hinder the process of communication. For example, the manager may ask an open question and be met only with silence; this negative response may prompt the manager to revert to previous procedures, and try to tell the subordinate what should be done, thus perpetuating dependence rather than encouraging independence. Open questions in fact have no implicit answers, and are used to stimulate reflection, promote discovery and exploration, and encourage thinking on the part of the subordinate. Ideally they start with: 'what', 'where', 'when', 'how', and 'who' ('why' questions can sometimes be seen as aggressive, particularly in the early stages of coaching). Closed questions are less useful because they only promote a 'yes' or a 'no' response. There are four specific types of open question:

- **Clarifying questions** are designed to generate specific information. For example: 'What precisely does that mean to you?'. Such questions can also help to confirm understanding, and are frequently asked in connection with mirroring, paraphrasing, or reflecting on what the person has said.

- **Creative questions** promote discovery and open up the mind to new possibilities. For example: 'How have you seen your colleagues handle similar situations?'.

- **Process questions** generate useful information about performance issues and problems, and allow the coach to manage the session in terms of structure. For example: 'What would you like to get from this session?' or 'What authority do you think you will need to complete this stage of the work?'.

- **Empathic questions** deal with the person's feelings about the effect of an event or a situation on them. Such questions convey empathy, generate trust and build the rapport so necessary to the success of performance coaching. They are asked for the purpose of expressing concern rather than finding solutions to problems. For example: 'How did you feel when that happened to you?'.

## GIVING CONSTRUCTIVE FEEDBACK

Active listening and good questioning techniques, as we have seen, enhance rapport and communication. Feedback completes the picture as it is the extent to which the manager and the subordinate are willing to be open, truthful, and to give relevant information about themselves or the situation to each other. The purpose of feedback from the manager's point of view is to assist the subordinate in maintaining or enhancing present levels of effectiveness, and to increase their self-awareness, particularly with regard to strengths and areas of improvement. Given properly, feedback results in greater rapport between the manager and the subordinate; it also offers options and encourages thought and decision-making. It can be positive and supportive (which reinforces effective and desirable behaviour), or negative and corrective (which indicates that change in ineffective or inappropriate behaviour is required). In this sense, all feedback is aimed at change; it can be done supportively or destructively.

## POSITIVE, SUPPORTIVE FEEDBACK

One of the most damaging assumptions that many managers make is that the only time feedback should be given is when the subordinate does something wrong, since good performance and appropriate behaviour are the expected norm. An axiom of effective management is, however, to observe the subordinate doing something right, and then acknowledge it. Managers should and do know when they are being supportive to their staff. If the manager focuses on what the subordinate is doing well, then the subordinate will concentrate on doing good work. What is reinforced has a tendency to become stronger. When people respond to the high expectations of their managers with high performance, that occurrence is called 'the effective cycle'.

Skinner (1953) has established that any acceptable change in behaviour can best be brought about through positive rather than negative reinforcement. A positive reinforcer (praise, encouragement, reward) tends to strengthen the response it follows and makes that response more likely to occur in the future. In other words, when desirable behaviour is achieved by the subordinate it must be rewarded as soon as possible. This strategy is compatible with the concept of setting short-term goals, as well as final performance criteria, and then reinforcing appropriate progress towards the desired behaviour. When thinking about giving positive reinforcers, the manager should remember that reinforcement depends on the individual subordinate, as what is reinforcing to one might not be reinforcing to another. Also, the same person at different times will be motivated by different things, as we have seen, depending on present need satisfaction. Thus, at one time a person might respond to praise as a reinforcer, but at another time that same person might not respond to praise but be very eager to take on more responsibility. The manager as coach, therefore, must be cognizant of the dangers of overgeneralizing and not only look for unique differences in their staff but also be aware of the various changes in need satisfaction within the subordinate.

Feedback is effective when it is focused on a description of observed behaviour rather than on personality, and is based on specifics rather than on impressions: it should be consistent and well-timed, drawing attention to what the subordinate has done well – as well as suggesting avenues for improvement and help. It is often best if the manager discusses the characteristics of effective feedback with the subordinate before the start of the coaching session. That person then has the opportunity to discuss possible reactions to this sort of feedback. However they should also understand that the manager will follow up and give additional feedback when the situation warrants it.

## CRITICAL FEEDBACK
Feedback, of course, sometimes contains criticism. In fact, constructive criticism is sometimes as essential to the growth of the person's learning as supportive feedback. As we have seen previously, it should only be used to alter specifically identified behaviours that are seen to be ineffective or inappropriate. Some managers nevertheless feel apprehensive about giving even this kind of feedback, and some subordinates may feel defensive and embarrassed when receiving it. To ease matters, the manager should have an alternative idea available once the person being coached is aware of the inappropriate behaviour. By presenting the alternative immediately after the feedback, the manager helps the subordinate to save face and dignity, and to emerge from a potentially uncomfortable situation in the shortest possible time. The criticism must also be non-threatening and avoid casting the subordinate in the role of victim rather than that of someone who has made a mistake and is willing to accept and correct it. It should also be presented in a context that allows the person freedom to express any emotions they may be feeling. Such expression is important in building good, trusting relationships, as indicated earlier. Subordinates may, however, sometimes need help in expressing emotions constructively rather than destructively, and in a way that enhances rather than threatens the manager/subordinate relationship.

Pareek and Rao (1990) have outlined some examples of unhelpful, defensive reactions to feedback as follows:

- **Denying** instead of accepting responsibility for the behaviour being discussed.

- **Rationalizing** instead of analysing why the behaviour occurred.

- **Assuming** that the manager supplying the feedback has negative feelings about the subordinate.

- **Expressing negative feelings** instead of exploring the feedback with the manager.

- **Accepting feedback automatically** and without exploration instead of eliciting more information in order to understand it more fully.

- **Taking an aggressive stand** towards the manager instead of seeking help in understanding the feedback.

- **Displaying humour and wit** instead of concern for improvement.

- **Exhibiting 'counter dependence'** i.e. rejecting the manager's authority.

- **Showing cynicism or scepticism** about improvement instead of accepting the feedback; this includes a tendency to plan to check it with other people later on.

- **Generalizing** instead of experimenting with alternatives for improvement.

## FEEDBACK ABOUT ONESELF: 'SELF-DISCLOSURE'

Feedback in relation to others is, of course, just one side of the coin. The other side involves providing feedback about oneself – that is, self-disclosure (the ability to talk truthfully and fully about oneself) – which is another vital factor in effective communication. An individual cannot really communicate with another person or get to know that person well unless they can engage in self-disclosure, and that self-disclosure should be a mutual process: 'The more I know about you, and the more you know about me, the more effective and efficient will be our communication'. An individual's ability to engage in self-revelation is a symptom of a healthy personality; to know oneself and to have satisfying interpersonal relationships one must be able to reveal oneself to others. However, many people have fears and doubts about self-disclosure, often stemming from worries that they will not be totally accepted, that parts of themselves will be unlovable or that they are unworthy as people. Cautious, ritualized communication is the result. For such people, and ideally for others as well, disclosure can only be communicated in an atmosphere of trust and goodwill.

## GIVING FEEDBACK

### EXERCISE 10

*When you provide feedback to a subordinate, do you tend to do the following?*

- Clarify what you want to say to the person in advance and get all the facts you need.

- Start with positives so that the person sees that you are not dismissing all their performance; acknowledge successes.

- Select important areas for feedback – don't nit-pick.

- Describe what you have seen in behavioural terms, not personality-based ones.

- Ask what happened when things have gone wrong and give the person the opportunity to explain before proceeding.

- Encourage and help the person to take full responsibility for their behaviour as appropriate.

- Help the person to see the probable consequences and help them to learn from the experience so as to reduce the possibility of recurrence.

- Support the person in the development of an action plan to deal with any current issues.

- Show confidence in the person and end the session with positives about the future.

*THE JOHARI WINDOW*

It is through feedback and constructive criticism that the subordinate comes to know how the manager regards the work they have done. A useful model to help formalize the process of thinking through how feedback and constructive criticism might best be offered, is known as the Johari Window (the term 'Johari' is formed by an amalgam of the abbreviated first names of the authors, Joseph Luft and Harry Ingham (Luft 1970)). The Johari Window can be looked at as a communication window through which information is given and received about self and others, as follows:

|  | Known to self | Unknown to self |
|---|---|---|
| Known to others | PUBLIC | BLIND |
| Unknown to others | PRIVATE | UNKNOWN |

The Johari Window (Luft, 1970)

The arena that is *known to self* and also *known to others* in any specific organizational setting is called the **public** arena – it is known to all. The arena that is *unknown to self* but is *known to others* is referred to as the **blind** area. The area that is *known to self* but *unknown to others* is referred to as the **private** area. The last area, *unknown to self* and *unknown to others*, is called the **unknown** area. There are two processes that affect the shape of this window: the first is **feedback** (the extent to which others are willing to share) and the second is **disclosure** (the extent to which the self is willing to share with others data about themselves).

Let us consider this window in terms of the coaching process from the perspective of both the manager and the subordinate, in the table opposite (adapted from Luft, 1970).

Looking at the four sections of the window from the manager's perspective in terms of columns and rows, the two columns represent the manager and the two rows represent the subordinate. There are some attitudes and behaviours engaged in by both manager and subordinate that are open to everyone. Column 1 contains 'Things the manager knows about himself' and Column 2 contains 'Things the manager does not know about himself/herself'. Row 1 contains 'Things that the subordinate knows about the manager' and Row 2 contains 'Things that the subordinate does not know about the manager'.

The information contained in these rows and columns is not static but moves from one area to another as the level of mutual trust and the exchange of feedback varies in and during the length of the coaching process sessions. As a consequence of this movement, the size and shape of the sections within the window will vary.

## The manager's Johari Window

|  | Things I know | Things I don't know |
|---|---|---|
| **Things they know** | *Public arena*<br>• What the task is.<br><br>• Action plan (e.g. reporting stages).<br>• Praise/constructive criticism. | *Blind area*<br>• How I communicate my feelings about the subordinate's ability.<br>• My view of the importance/lack of importance of the task.<br><br>*(This is an area where feedback from the subordinate would be helpful)* |
| **Things they don't know** | *Private area*<br>• What doubts do I have about the subordinate's ability?<br>• Why I am coaching this subordinate at this time?<br>• Why have I chosen this task to delegate at this time?<br>*(This is an area where disclosure to the subordinate would be helpful.)* | *Unknown area*<br>• The impact of failure.<br><br>• Organizational consequences of success/failure.<br>• My views of personality. |

## The subordinate's Johari Window

|  | Things I know | Things I don't know |
|---|---|---|
| **Things they know** | *Public arena*<br>• What the task is.<br><br>• Action plan (e.g. reporting stages).<br><br>• My questions. | *Blind area*<br>• My expression of my emotional reaction to the task.<br>• My non-verbal expression of my view of the interest/importance of the task.<br>*(This is an area where feedback from the manager would be helpful.)* |
| **Things they don't know** | *Private area*<br>• What if I am not able to do it (fear of failure)?<br>• My real understanding of the task.<br><br>*(This is an area where disclosure to the manager would be helpful.)* | *Unknown area*<br>• The impact of failure.<br><br>• Organizational consequences of success/failure.<br>• Impact on my career. |

The Johari Window (Adapted from Luft, 1970. Reprinted with permission.)

The first section, called the open arena or **public arena**, contains things that the manager knows about himself and about which the subordinate knows. This arena includes all free and open exchange of information and observable behaviour (though not the motives, unless they are honestly communicated). This arena increases in size as the level of trust and rapport increases and as information is shared in a supportive communication climate.

The second section, the **blind area**, contains information that the manager does not know or of which he is not aware. As the manager begins to participate in the coaching sessions, he will communicate all kinds of information of which he is not aware, but which is being picked up by the subordinate. This information, as we have seen, may be in the form of verbal or non-verbal cues, like mannerisms, the way something is said, or the style in which things are related to the subordinate. The extent to which the manager can be insensitive to their own behaviour and what it may appear to communicate to the subordinate can be quite surprising and disconcerting. For example, I once had a manager who, every time he had something to complain about, would stand with his back to the radiator in front of the same window, clearing his throat three or four times to get attention before saying something about what he didn't like.

In the section the **private area** are things the manager knows about himself but of which the subordinate is directly unaware. For one reason or another, the manager keeps this information hidden: it could be for fear that if the subordinate knew of these feelings, perceptions and opinions, the subordinate might reject, attack, hurt or lose respect for the manager. As a consequence the manager withholds the information in his communication with the subordinate. One of the reasons the manager keeps this information hidden is that no supportive evidence from the subordinate is observable to disclose it. The manager assumes that if those feelings and reactions were revealed, the subordinate might judge negatively. However, in the coaching process, the manager will never know how the subordinate would react unless the assumptions are put to the test by revealing something of how things are viewed. In other words, if the manager does not take some risks, the reality or unreality of the assumptions will never be known. On the other hand, the manager may want to keep certain kinds of information hidden when the motives for doing so are to keep power, be in control or to manipulate others.

The last section – the **unknown** – contains things that neither the manager nor the subordinate knows. Some of this material may be so far below the surface that their existence is never known. Other material, for example, early childhood memories, unrecognized resources, may be below the surface but, through an exchange of feedback, may be made public. Of course, since knowing all about oneself is highly unlikely, part of this section will always remain unknown or 'unconscious'.

One goal the manager can set for himself or herself in the coaching process is to decrease the blind area section. Since this section contains information that the subordinate knows, but of which the manager is unaware, the only way to increase awareness of this information is to get feedback from the subordinate by the manager developing a receptive attitude to solicit and encourage the subordinate to be forthcoming and to give feedback in such a way that it does not seem like criticism. The more the manager encourages this feedback the more the line in the window will move to the right.

Another goal the manager can set within the coaching process is to reduce the 'hidden or private' area, which contains information kept from the subordinate, by giving feedback of reactions to what is felt by the manager in terms of perceptions and opinions thus obviating the necessity on the part of the subordinate to guess, interpret or project what the manager's behaviour means. Disclosure is the extent to which the manager and the subordinate are willing to share with each other those aspects of themselves which are relevant to the working environment. The more information that the two sides disclose to each other about the way they see, hear, think, feel, behave and react, the more the public arena takes over, and the smaller the private area becomes. In addition, through the process of giving and receiving feedback, new information, inspiration and insight can result, but as we have seen, it is not an easy task, and sometimes can be construed as evaluative and judgemental.

Since all managers are responsible for making their people 'winners', the role the manager as coach plays in the development cycle of their staff, and how the skills of effective communication towards achieving the identified responsibilities and outcomes of good performance are used, cannot be too strongly emphasized.

In this chapter the conditions and skills involved in effective coaching have been discussed. Chapter 5 outlines an actual coaching programme.

To summarize:

❑ Coaching is particularly applicable for someone who is new to a job, or where there is possibility for growth in the job, where someone can learn from another's success, where someone can learn from failure or where there is a specific performance shortfall or problem.

❑ Coaching is not applicable in some parts of a manager's job (for instance, handling an attitude problem or activities such as long-range planning for organizational goals).

❑ Self-concept ('my psychological view of me') is a factor which helps or hinders both manager and subordinate in their communication with each other.

❑ Self-concept is a screen which filters all communication and may therefore help to avoid or promote defensive and other negative behaviours.

❑ Effective communication skills include an awareness of non-verbal behaviour, metacommunication, supportive and defensive communication, active listening, questioning techniques, feedback and criticism.

❑ Empathy has an impact on effective communication, which correlates well with productivity, satisfaction, good relationships and effective problem-solving.

❑ Factors in effective communication are the words themselves, the tone and other paralinguistic factors, and non-verbal behaviour.

❑ Many conditions block effective communication, including the preoccupation of the listener, other emotional states and past experiences. There are of course many other factors affecting relationships.

❑ Defensive communication aims at control and leads eventually to breakdown of communication and a deterioration in the relationship. Supportive communication, in contrast, is built on understanding and co-operation.

❑ Metacommunication goes beyond the straightforward verbal content of the message into the real meaning of the communication. There are many ways in which this can be expressed.

❑ Active listening involves listening for the full message, including what is expressed emotionally, and providing feedback that this has been heard and understood.

❑ Neuro-linguistic programming suggests that rapport between people makes communication flow easily and that rapport is an awareness of the total context of the verbal and non-verbal messages in the communication.

❏ Pacing and leading are critical factors in communication and in building rapport.

❏ The types of question to avoid in the coaching situation include critical questions, sarcastic questions, testing or leading questions. Open questions tend to be more useful than closed ones.

❏ Feedback is the final thread in the tapestry of good communication and rapport with positive reinforcement rather than punishment being more likely to bring about change in behaviour.

❏ When criticism forms a part of feedback, it should be non-threatening and should provide alternatives. Freedom to express emotions should be allowed although this should be done constructively. This will help to avoid unhelpful, defensive reactions to feedback.

❏ Self-disclosure helps to make communication effective and efficient, as it indicates a healthy personality and one which can avoid cautious, ritualized communication. The Johari Window is one model which helps to show how feedback, criticism and self-disclosure can be analyzed.

# *The Coaching Programme*

We now come to the coaching programme itself and the steps required to develop the subordinate's ability to achieve higher or improved performance. But the coaching process, done well, not only provides support for subordinates, it also gives managers a chance to evaluate themselves – in particular to examine their styles of leadership and their relationships with their staff. A good coaching programme needs to be carried out in a supportive, positive atmosphere, and one in which differences between individuals, such as thinking and decision-making styles, and conflict and emotional behaviour, can be recognized, accepted and used positively.

The coaching situation also requires the manager and the subordinate to work closely together. Sometimes the two of them may find it difficult to work in such close proximity from the point of view of temperament. More often a personality conflict, as mentioned in Chapter 2, is only a small part of the problem. Relationships involve mutual dependence between two fallible human beings. If the manager as coach fails to recognize this, they will either avoid trying to manage the relationship altogether or will manage it ineffectively.

Managing a situation of mutual dependence requires in particular a *good understanding* of the other person and oneself, especially regarding strengths, weaknesses, work styles and needs. Also, it requires the *ability to use this understanding* to develop and manage a healthy working relationship, compatible with the work styles and strengths of all concerned, characterized by mutual expectations and the satisfaction of each person's most critical needs. Such a relationship accommodates differences in work style but also allows and encourages subordinates to adjust their styles where necessary in response to their manager's preferred method of receiving information or making decisions: for example, some managers prefer information in report form, others for it to be presented in person so they can ask questions. Some managers prefer to be involved in decisions and problems as they arise, others prefer to deal with them at a time of their own choosing.

### Attributes of a good coaching programme

A good coaching programme:

- Creates a personal learning agenda where each coaching session builds on insights, experiences and past learning.

- Provides the skills and understanding to allow the subordinate to grow and develop in specific competencies, and to stretch mental abilities with practical, active learning methods and on-the-job experience.

- Helps the subordinate to gain a detailed grasp of management principles and problems, and develops abilities in innovative thinking.

- Leads to a better understanding by the subordinate of the scale and complexity of the events that influence the business situation, the elements outside their immediate experience, and the role of decison-making and intuition.

- Involves a variety of methods of learning including discussion, individual study and research, creative and analytical problem-solving, and all of the skills discussed in Chapter 4.

- Improves the subordinate's ability to develop commitment to the successful implementation of organizational strategy and its sustaining through any difficult times.

# THE COACHING PLAN

I will now go into the detail of the five-step coaching plan. After each step you will find an exercise which you can complete with a particular subordinate in mind so that at the end of the chapter you will be ready to start the discussion with them.There are five essential steps:

1. **Determine** the reasons for coaching and decide on the topic.

2. **Identify** long- and short-term goals; define targets and standards.

3. **Devise and develop** specific overall and individual 'session' plans.

4. **Develop** subordinate competence and confidence.

5. **Recap** on what has been agreed, set deadlines and check progress.

Let us now look at each step in detail.

## STEP 1: DETERMINE THE REASONS FOR COACHING AND DECIDE ON THE TOPIC

As discussed in Chapter 4, there are many circumstances in which the manager will need to coach someone on their staff. In the main, these occur when a subordinate has been promoted or, alternatively, has experienced a shortfall in performance, where there is a specific problem to solve, or where there is an opportunity to help the person grow. Often the subordinate who has been promoted is conscientious and capable, but needs help in certain directions. If the manager tries to take over, take work away, or force a solution by dictating which way a job should be done, the subordinate could experience a lack of self-esteem, feel threatened, upset, cheated, or even devalued. Sherwood and Holyman (1978) suggest that there are certain factors to consider when deciding whether to assign a particular task to an individual:

1. The **nature of the task** itself – this is the first and most important criterion in determining whether a problem would best be solved by this particular person, by someone else, or by a group. Certain types of task, such as creative or independent tasks, may best be performed by individuals, other types of task that involve the integration of different functions are obviously particularly appropriate for groups.

2. The **importance** of the task solution.

3. The value placed on the **quality of the solution**.

4. The **competence of the person** and the time needed to find and implement the solution.

5. The **operating effectiveness of the person** concerned.

Once the decision has been made to assign a task to a subordinate, it is important that the manager introduces the task in a non-threatening way. It is also important to ask open questions to explore the subordinate's attitude towards, and thinking about, the task since their commitment to it is a vital component. In order to gain this commitment to the task, the manager must ensure the subordinate realizes from the outset that the task assigned, together with the authority and responsibility associated with it, will be theirs when the coaching sessions are completed. The coaching process which prepares the subordinate for (or is an integral part of) the task thus demands considerable commitment from both manager *and* subordinate. As we have seen, there are elements of risk and exposure inherent in the process, and the manager also has to take professional responsibility for deciding which part of the subordinate's job is to be influenced by the coaching. One of the goals of coaching is to help the subordinate develop and grow in the organization, but often a subordinate does not ask for coaching, and is, in effect, forced into it. When coaching is given unsought the manager has particular responsibility for the outcomes, and for the influence they have upon someone's present career and future prospects. A high quality of communication at the outset can reduce this unacceptable risk.

In determining the reasons for coaching and in setting the topic, the manager must never lose sight of the fact that the aim is to help the subordinate improve individual strengths and overcome weaknesses and difficulties. It should also be remembered that, as no one likes to be told about weaknesses, the best approach is to help the subordinate to discover these for themselves. The coaching topic should therefore be chosen and delivered in a way that helps the subordinate to investigate various dimensions of a problem, to discover any related but previously unidentified issues, and to voice any concerns. It should also be designed to encourage the subordinate to function independently. Sometimes subordinates are so loyal (and the manager so protective) that they become totally dependent on the manager, and from time to time the manager needs to reflect on whether this kind of relationship is being fostered unintentionally.

Once decisions have been taken on the reasons for coaching and the topic concerned, it is important to ensure that the subordinate understands these and has no unrealistic expectations or resentment at being given what they could see as an extra workload. This allows the subordinate to enter coaching in the right frame of

## STEP 1: THE REASONS FOR COACHING AND THE TOPIC

EXERCISE 11

Who is the subordinate? .......................................................
...................................................................................................
...................................................................................................

What is the reason for coaching this subordinate? (For example, a performance shortfall; a new skill; new knowledge; problem-solving, etc.) ...........................................................
...................................................................................................
...................................................................................................

What is the task? (For example: to develop . . . ; to implement . . . ; etc.) .......................................................................
...................................................................................................
...................................................................................................

What will the impact on performance/potential be from the subordinate's point of view – i.e. what's in it for them besides extra workload? .............................................................
...................................................................................................
...................................................................................................

What particular strengths does the subordinate bring to this situation? ........................................................................
...................................................................................................
...................................................................................................

Do you have to make special arrangements before the subordinate can start? (Such as access to information, communication with or support from other managers, staff, branches, sites.) ............................................................................
...................................................................................................
...................................................................................................

Can the subordinate function independently, or are there areas in the coaching project where they will have to hand over to you or to other managers, individuals or groups? ........
...................................................................................................
...................................................................................................

mind. McCormack (1993) suggests that in further encouraging this attitude, subtle forms of persuasion are more effective and less wearisome than those which are demanding and dictating. Subtle persuasion often involves dropping coaching ideas in the person's lap and then helping them to notice these ideas, or convincing the subordinate that the ideas come from them rather than from the manager.

## STEP 2: IDENTIFY LONG- AND SHORT-TERM GOALS; DEFINE TARGETS AND STANDARDS

Step 2 is easier if the manager can identify at least two opportunities in the near future when coaching will be needed. They should also decide on the timescale for its completion as well as define which tasks actually require coaching. The manager also needs to identify realistic, achievable and measurable goals (by quality, quantity, cost and/or time) for the coaching and, probably for each individual coaching session. This helps in the monitoring of the programme.

Before beginning the programme the manager has to decide how well the subordinate is doing currently, how able and willing they are to take on the responsibility, and where information can be obtained to help make these judgements. Much of this information may come directly from observation of the subordinate's behaviour. For example, they can be asked how well they think they are doing at specific tasks, how they respond to the idea of taking on more responsibility and work in the first instance, and what their aims and ambitions are in both the short and long term. Obviously, with some subordinates, asking for their own assessment of their readiness won't be productive, but most people are aware of how they are doing in their work and are able to share this kind of information. Their ability, as well as their attitudes and willingness, can also be determined by examining how they have performed in the past.

Other questions the manager can usefully consider are: 'Does this person have the necessary knowledge to perform well in the area, and do they know what needs to be done?'; 'What is their interest level?'; 'What is their commitment in this area?'; 'Is the person's self-confidence secure in this area, or do they lack confidence and feel insecure?'

## STEP 2: LONG- AND SHORT-TERM GOALS; TARGETS AND STANDARDS

### EXERCISE 12

When do you estimate that the coaching process will be finished? ...................................................................................

When can the subordinate first start practising the new skills? ...................................................................................

Are there likely to be other occasions in the near future?
...................................................................................
...................................................................................

What goals/targets/standards do you want to discuss with the subordinate? ...........................................................................
...................................................................................
...................................................................................

How well do you think the subordinate measures up to the challenges of these goals in terms of:
(a) knowledge? ...................................................................
(b) skills? ...........................................................................
(c) attitude? .......................................................................
...................................................................................

Which of the subordinate's past achievements give you confidence that the coaching will be a success? ....................
...................................................................................
...................................................................................

What are your goals for the first meeting with the subordinate to discuss this project? (For example, to excite interest? Lay down ground rules, etc.) ....................................................
...................................................................................
...................................................................................

Does the project break down easily into separate steps? If so, can you develop a detailed plan for the coaching process?
...................................................................................
...................................................................................

What do you plan to do to capitialize on the learning which takes place at each stage? ....................................................
...................................................................................
...................................................................................

The subordinate's 'readiness level' gives a good clue to how to begin. For example, the manager may need to start by being a little directive, or by being extra supportive, or by providing extra control and supervision.

As stated previously, the ideal coaching situation allows the person to complete a task which the manager has assigned while at the same time strengthening their skills. Few people achieve success immediately. As a result, the manager as coach should look for opportunities to reward any small progress made in the desired direction. Increased responsibility should be assigned in appropriate stages – too much all at once may result in failure – and rewards given as each short-term goal is achieved on the way to long-term success. Within the coaching process, learning should be an explicit target, pursued as consciously and deliberately as profit or productivity.

## STEP 3: DEVISE AND DEVELOP SPECIFIC OVERALL AND INDIVIDUAL 'SESSION' PLANS

The success of this step depends in part upon discovering the subordinate's preferred learning style. The manager should review the four styles described in Chapter 4 with the specific person in mind, and decide which one appears most appropriate. In doing so, the subordinate's opinion should also, in most cases, be sought. The next part of Step 3 is to devise a clear plan of action for the person to take on this task. The plan should allow for the subordinate's preferred learning style, and enable the manager to vary their coaching according to the various elements required in the task – i.e. the skill and knowledge demanded and the parameters imposed by it. Decisions may also have to be taken on the authority and power needed by the subordinate to carry out the task. This may mean ensuring that colleagues are aware of the task and the subordinate's role in it, and will co-operate and allow access to resources such as data, administrative support and possibly expense items.

After completing these arrangements, the manager can prepare questions designed to help the subordinate focus on and diagnose the specific problems involved in the task, and to think of possible solutions to them. These solutions can then be discussed, with the manager only offering suggestions if it seems appropriate or if the person being coached has clearly run out of ideas. After solutions have been generated, the manager can help the subordinate

# STAGE 3: OVERALL AND INDIVIDUAL 'SESSION' PLANS

## EXERCISE 13

What do you think is the subordinate's preferred learning style? (If you have not already observed it, try using the case studies in Chapter 4.) ........................................................

What is your own preferred learning style? (If they are not the same, pay particular attention to the next stage of this process.) ................................................................................

What are some of the potential pitfalls which might be caused by the subordinate's learning style in this particular project? (For example, moving in without adequate forethought?) ........

What is your plan of action to control progress? (Note that in the actual performance, the subordinate should be encouraged to develop their own plan for accomplishment; you should stay in the background.) .........................................,

Does this involve a different level of decision-making or authority for the subordinate? If so, how do you plan to discuss this? ...............................................................

What is your role going to be in terms of support? (For instance, the provision of information, arranging for extra travel or expenses, etc.) ...............................................................

What questions will help the subordinate to focus on and diagnose the specific problems that they are likely to encounter? (You will need open-ended questions.) ................

A word of advice: *when you discuss these with your subordinate, let them comment on options, advantages and disadvantages first. If you give your views first your experience and knowledge is likely to dominate or even to block the subordinate's thinking. Your aim is to provoke their thinking. (You may also learn something new yourself, of course!)*

to assess the advantages and disadvantages of each of them, to raise questions about their feasibility, to choose between them, and to finalize a step-by-step action plan. This action plan should be sufficiently flexible to be revised after the implementation stage in response to whatever contingencies may occur.

## STEP 4: DEVELOP SUBORDINATE COMPETENCE AND CONFIDENCE

All the skills mentioned in Chapter 4 should be used in this step, for example: establishing rapport, choosing the appropriate environment for the coaching sessions; watching body language; and communicating effectively. The subordinate's competence and confidence can then be helped by:

- using **active listening** skills
- using **questions** to draw out solutions
- inviting the subordinate to **evaluate** these solutions
- drawing out the **consequences** of each of them
- **building** on the subordinate's ideas and suggestions
- **suspending** judgement
- **sharing** experience
- **exhausting** the flow of the subordinate's ideas/suggestions before offering comments
- **paraphrasing** the subordinate's contributions to ensure full understanding
- summarizing and checking to **clarify** what has been agreed
- giving supportive **feedback**.

Confidence and competence are also helped by specifying clearly what constitutes good performance in each area, so that subordinates know exactly what is expected of them and can recognize when their performance is approaching the desired level. Managers cannot change and develop their subordinates' behaviour in areas that are unclear. The development of a subordinate's competence and confidence should also be seen within the context of their broad career development. Professional and personal life go through cycles of growth, stability and transition. Each of these cycles or stages involves the resolution of important psychological issues, and central to these in professional life is the process of change. Both the manager's and the subordinate's job skills and career aspirations develop and alter over time, with those experiences in the early years of a career influencing later aspirations.

Schein (1971) developed the concept of a 'career cone', and argued that individuals' careers in organizations can develop along three directions: vertically, horizontally and radially. The most common type of career move is along the hierarchical or vertical dimension. People obtain promotions and rise to levels of increasing leadership within the organization. Although many people pursue the same job function or technical speciality throughout their careers, others switch their functions or specialities, often changing the breadth of their responsibilities in the process.

When considering Step 4 in the coaching process, the manager should ideally take into account the subordinate's likely career movement. If it is not vertical, it may be radial, i.e. it may involve movement towards the inner circle of the organization, gaining increased access to special privileges and organizational 'secrets' about future business decisions and personnel decisions, or, perhaps as in the case of an older colleague, the subordinate may be moving away from the inner circle. Alternatively, the person may be moving horizontally, taking on new duties and tasks but without necessarily increasing responsibility or status.

Whatever the movement of a subordinate's career, Step 4 may also need to take into account the *stage* through which they are passing. Dalton *et al.* (1977) identify four stages, namely: apprentice, colleague, mentor and sponsor. At the *apprentice stage* individuals are relatively dependent on their managers for training: their work is primarily technical and they are learning to apply previous knowledge (i.e. formal education, previous employment and experience) to their present tasks. At the *colleague stage*, they are expected to work more independently, to make contributions to the organization and to work well with colleagues. At the *mentor stage*, they are required to take on more responsibility for others, and at the *sponsor stage*, they have to extend their responsibilities from controlling and developing subordinates to managing the growth and development of the organization. Most managers themselves are at the mentor stage and most subordinates, at the apprentice or colleague stage, but this is by no means invariable.

Arnold and Feldman (1986) suggest that this four-stage career model can be broken down into smaller, more discrete stages

## Four-stage career model

| Age group | Career group | Career tasks | Psychological issues |
|---|---|---|---|
| 15–22 | Pre-career: exploration. | Finding the right one. Obtaining the appropriate education. | Discovering one's own needs and interests. Developing a realistic self-assessment of one's abilities. |
| 22–30 | Early career: trial. | Obtaining a viable first job. Adjusting to daily work routines and managers. | Overcoming the insecurity of experience: developing self-confidence. Learning to get along with others in a work setting. |
| 30–38 | Early career: establishment. | Choosing a special area of competence. Becoming an independent contributor to the organization. | Deciding on level of professional and organization commitment. Dealing with feelings of failure of first independent projects or assignments. |
| 38–45 | Middle-career: transition. | Reassessing one's true career abilities, talents and interests. Withdrawing from one's own mentor and preparing to become a mentor to others. | Reassessing one's progress relative to one's ambitions. Resolving work-life/personal-life conflicts. |
| 45–55 | Middle career: growth. | Being a mentor. Taking on more responsibilities for general management. | Dealing with the competitiveness and aggression of younger persons on the 'fast track' up the organization. Learning to substitute wisdom-based experience for immediate technical skills. |

*(Other writers suggest that lack of promotability may also become an issue at this point.)*

| | | | |
|---|---|---|---|
| 55–62 | Late career: maintenance. | Making strategic decisions about the future of the business. Becoming concerned with the broader role of the organisation in civic and political arenas. | Becoming primarily concerned with the organization's welfare rather than one's own career. Handling highly political or important decisions without becoming emotionally upset. |
| 62–70 | Late career: withdrawal. | Selecting and developing key subordinates for future leadership roles. Accepting reduced levels of power and responsibility. | Finding new sources of life satisfaction outside the job. Maintaining a sense of self-worth without a job. |

From Arnold and Feldman, 1986. *Organisational Behavior*, McGraw-Hill Inc. (Reprinted with permission.)

that apply to most occupations. The table on page 99 represents a summary of their proposals.

Individuals need both to master work activities and to resolve important psychological issues at each point in their careers, and in Step 4 the coach needs to keep this in mind in order to tailor the coaching programme to the particular needs of the subordinate concerned. By understanding the nature of career stages and choices, the manager can predict how productive, willing and able subordinates will be during the coaching programme, and can anticipate the problems and opportunities likely to arise more effectively.

---

## STEP 4: DEVELOPING SUBORDINATE COMPETENCE AND CONFIDENCE

### EXERCISE 14

What will constitute good performance in each area of the project to be assigned? ............................................................
........................................................................................................
........................................................................................................
........................................................................................................

What will this contribute to the subordinate's career development? (Note that this does not necessarily mean upward movement. For example, one person can make a career as a weight-lifter while another can become a supervisor, a manager or a director of weight-lifters.) ...................................
........................................................................................................
........................................................................................................
........................................................................................................

Which life stage does the subordinate occupy?
(Which age group or career group: i.e. apprentice, colleague, mentor or sponsor? See text for details.) ...................................
........................................................................................................
........................................................................................................
........................................................................................................

How are you going to create an atmosphere that will minimize the risk of failure? ...........................................................................
........................................................................................................
........................................................................................................
........................................................................................................

## STEP 5: RECAP ON WHAT HAS BEEN AGREED, SET DEADLINES AND CHECK PROGRESS

Both the manager and the subordinate have a mutual commitment to making the coaching sessions work by jointly:

- Being clear about what is required in terms of specific, identifiable outcomes.

- Making an overall summary of major learning points.

- Recapping at the end of each session to make sure everything is clear.

- Setting deadlines and confirming actions for each part of the task.

- Agreeing an implementation plan as regards reasonable time schedules for the completion of the various tasks.

- Having review sessions regularly to check progress and achievement.

Adequate follow-up is important, as even good coaching sessions will ultimately fail if it is omitted. The coach should work out a system to provide specific support at each stage of the programme, as well as systems for monitoring the implementation and for following up. If the manager fails to follow up, the subordinate may feel that the coaching was artificial and in consequence may lose interest in improving performance.

Chapter 4 dealt with constructive feedback, and here it is only necessary to mention the need for support when the subordinate has achieved the objectives and goals set for the programme. The following steps are suggested by Karp (1987) as a strategy for this supportive feedback:

❑ **Acknowledge the specific action and result to be reinforced.** The subordinate should know immediately that the coach is pleased with what they have done. Feedback should be specific, and describe the event in behavioural terms. For example: 'You finished the tasks (*action*) on time (*result*)'.

❑ **Explain the effects of the accomplishment and offer appreciation.** The effects of the subordinate's behaviour should be identified in specific, observable ways. Appreciation is important, but drawing attention to results is even more so. 'It was a major

## STEP 5: RECAP, SET DEADLINES, CHECK PROGRESS

### EXERCISE 15

There are two stages to be carried out:

At the end of the face-to-face session with the subordinate you will need to ensure that you both agree on . . .

- what is required
- why the coaching is being undertaken
- what the subordinate can expect to learn
- what the advantages will be
- what the deadlines and time schedules are.

In addition, you will need to:
- set up progress and review sessions
- plan ahead for debriefing at the end of the project
- give specific positive feedback and specific negative feedback if necessary
- draw out learning points
- ensure that the subordinate realizes their role in achieving the success

*Well done coach! It's not easy, but I am sure that you will have found it rewarding – and your subordinate certainly will.*

factor in getting the contract (*result*) and I am pleased with your outstanding work (*appreciation*).'

❑ **Help the subordinate to take full responsibility for the success.** If the subordinate acknowledges the feedback, this step is accomplished. If they seem over-modest, more work is needed. Unless the subordinate can internalize the success and receive satisfaction from it to some degree, very little growth is likely to occur. In talking about what happened, the subordinate should be helped to realize how much they were responsible for the result. It is important for both the manager and the subordinate to hear and acknowledge how the success was accomplished.

❑ **Ask if the subordinate wants to talk about anything else.** While the subordinate is feeling positive and knows that they are recognized and appreciated, they may be receptive enough to open up on other issues.

❏ **Thank the subordinate for the good performance.** This final step assures that the coach's appreciation will be uppermost in the subordinate's mind on leaving the session and returning to work.

## THE IMPORTANCE OF INVOLVEMENT

In conclusion, at one level subordinates have always been involved merely by virtue of being employed – but employee involvement in today's terms necessitates more than this. It involves a fundamental shift in attitude from viewing staff as operatives to viewing them as people with valued skills, talents and experiences who want to do excellent work and to contribute to the well-being of the department and organization in which they work. A final list of questions should help managers to make this shift:

- How clearly do your subordinates understand their roles?

- Are they appreciated for what they do? By you? By others?

- Are they obtaining the information they need to do a good job?

- What ideas do they have about their future in the department or organization?

- Do they understand clearly the direction of the organization for which they work?

- Are they consulted when decisions are made in areas in which they have experience and expertise?

Coaching is an excellent way of changing the way people work, approach and think about, as well as grow in their jobs. It helps them want to give their best because they are encouraged and supported, and their ideas are listened to. The manager's key role as coach is to support and develop their subordinates. The most important reward for managers is knowing that they have helped someone to develop and succeed. Coaching is the oil on the wheels of change. The impetus for change comes from managers themselves who have the power to drive the coaching initiative. Coaching is a difficult, intense task for the manager; it requires patience and the use of several skills but produces many rewards. Over time it enhances subordinates' strengths, minimizes their weaknesses or corrects areas for improvement, and helps them realize their full potential, thereby benefiting them, the manager, and the organization as a whole.

Coaching is about developing staff in their present jobs, not just about up-dating their knowledge. It is a matter of helping them to expand their capabilities and develop their full potential and talents in their present jobs, not just in the hope of promotion if and when a vacancy arises. In other words, it is helping staff to grow and to think for themselves, to be self-reliant, and to gain confidence to tackle more responsibility and accept bigger challenges.

Coaching is very much part of the manager's job: he or she needs to have, as well as to show, confidence in subordinates in order to delegate tasks – tasks which will make them more capable and more satisfied in their jobs, which in turn will allow them to demonstrate to themselves that they are capable of taking on extra responsibilities.

As we have seen, managers do have misconceptions about coaching. They equate it with on-the-job training or with promotion, and may see no point in developing staff in a real sense. Coaching helps staff to make a greater contribution to the organization's work although it does involve the manager in taking risks to encourage learning in subordinates. These risks can be minimized, however, by briefing the subordinate carefully, by warning them of potential dangers, and by helping them to weigh up the pros and cons of certain actions. Ultimately they can then make decisions, carry out negotiations and, in the debriefing with the manager, go over the learning experience and identify what could have been done better or what other options there were.

## Effective coaching

To coach effectively the manager must:

- Know which tasks can be delegated that will help the subordinate to take on managerial jobs more effectively and efficiently.

- Know at what level the subordinate is, at the present time, in terms of knowledge, experience and formal training.

- Know where the subordinate needs to be developed; where using the day-to-day work of the department can be used as a learning experience.

- Actively seek for coaching opportunities to develop subordinates.

- Believe that there are coaching opportunities at all times and not just when there is a problem.

- Be prepared to delegate important tasks that stretch the subordinate, and not just routine tasks which provide no real learning experience.

- Ensure that the subordinate has learned from the experience by asking the right questions, encouraging the person to think and decide for themselves, appraising results and acknowledging work well done.

- Ensure that subordinates work out their own problems, and do not run to the manager each time they find difficulties or when something goes wrong.

- Refrain from blaming the subordinate if they make a mistake, but rather analyse where improvements can be made, and what can be learned from the mistake.

To summarize:

❏ Manager and subordinate are in a situation of mutual dependency which has certain specific requirements, and to which coaching can add value.

❏ Our coaching plan has five steps:
  - determine the reasons for coaching and decide on the topic
  - identify long- and short-term goals: define targets and standards
  - devise and develop specific overall and individual 'session' plans
  - develop subordinate confidence and competence
  - recap what has been agreed; set deadlines and check progress.

❏ The work plan for each step is to be found in the *Exercises*.

❏ Staff are often people with valued skills, talents, knowledge and experiences who are committed to their work and the organization.

❏ Coaching helps to achieve the result of increased productivity and motivation by providing encouragement, support and development.

❏ Coaching focuses on the development in the present job and the coaching process is a significant part of the manager's job.

# CONCLUSION

You have read about the main aims and benefits of coaching and its impact on the organization in this book. The exercises and the coaching model have given you 'hands-on' experience as far as is possible on a printed page. It is time to see where we have been and to look at what will happen as a result of your coaching activities.

We started our journey by determining the role of coaching in the achievement of organizational excellence. As we said in the first chapter, coaching helps in the marrying together of the two aspects of a manager's job – getting results through people. Two recent shifts in organizations point up the importance of the role of coaching. De-layering means that managers can no longer expect to control each subordinate with the degree of closeness which was possible in the more vertically structured organisations. Subordinates have to be taught (and trusted) to perform effectively on their own. A shift of emphasis towards teamwork in addition to enhanced individual contribution places a great importance on the self-confidence of subordinates as well as on their individual competence.

In the second chapter we turned our attention to matters of style and motivation. Personality and the impact of personal style are happy hunting grounds for many management educators who all have preferred models. The four styles presented here can easily be used to predict and to overcome communication problems in the coaching situation as well as to contribute to better relationships in general. Observation over a period of time is clearly needed to determine the best approach to an individual, but coaching provides an admirable opportunity to try out specific behaviours along the lines of those suggested. It is unlikely that the manager would be far wrong in the assessment made, and the results of applying an appropriate coaching style far outweigh the fear that the situation may have been incorrectly diagnosed.

Chapter 3 stressed the need for clearly structured action plans. Any coaching plan must include an assessment of the preferred learning style of the person being coached. The coach's own preferred style can have a considerable impact on how coaching is carried out, and time spent in gaining an awareness of one's own style is therefore time well spent. A meshing between what might be termed the coach's instructional style and the subordinate's preferred learning style, will have a major impact on the success of the coaching.

Coaching success is also clearly dependent on good communication, and other factors such as self-concept and empathy should not be forgotten, as was pointed out in Chapter 4. In addition to considering barriers to communication and investigating how to maintain an open communications climate, the importance of active listening in the understanding of the full message cannot be overstated. Coupled with a sensitivity to others, which can in part be achieved through Neuro-Linguistic Programming, the communication techniques discussed in this chapter will promote a positive, reinforcing climate where feedback is used as a two-way tool to improve results and relationships.

The final chapter pulled all the strands together to produce a specific coaching plan. The five steps of the plan demand a great deal of thinking and analysis, especially in the early stages of beginning a coaching programme, but this is justified by the resultant increases in productivity and motivation.

It is important not to forget that there are significant personal benefits for the coach in embarking on this long journey – it is not just the subordinate or the organization which will benefit. There are benefits for the coach's self-esteem such as the knowledge that they too may be thought of as role models in the future. There are also skill benefits for the coach – applying learning style theory to improve job understanding, improving listening habits, improving questioning and other communication techniques. Understanding of self and others provides another family of benefits to the coach – management styles and their impact, motivational theory, personality styles. The freeing of time in the longer term to enable the coach to work on higher level tasks is not the least of the benefits awaiting the manager who has the confidence in self and subordinates to start on the difficult but extremely rewarding journey of coaching. Growth, enhanced motivation, independence, increased productivity, enhanced teamwork – these are benefits to be seized avidly and are a natural result of the coaching process.

# REFERENCES

Arnold, H. J. and Feldman, D. C. (1986) *Organizational Behavior*. New York: McGraw-Hill.

Bandura, A. (1969) *Principles of Behavior Modification*. New York: Holt, Reinhardt & Winston.

Bass, B. M. and Avolio, B. J. (1994) *Improving Organizational Effectiveness*. Newbury Park, California: Sage Publications Inc.

Beggs, A. (1992) *Management Training*, May, 16.

Cooper, C. L. *et al.* (1988) *Living with Stress*. Harmondsworth: Penguin.

Dalton, G. Thompson, P. and Price, R. (1977) The four stages of professional careers: a new look at performance by professionals. *Organizational Dynamics*, 6, Summer 1977, 19–42.

Geier, J. G. and Downey, D. E. (1989) *Energetics of Personality*. Minnesota: Aristos Publishing House.

Gregory, C. (1994) The spice of life. London: *Upbeat*: Bupa/BLA Group Ltd. January, 8.

Handy, J. A. (1988) Theoretical and Methodological problems within Occupational Stress Burnout. *Human Relations*, 14:5, 351–369.

Herzberg, F. (1966) *Work and the Nature of Man*. New York: World Publications.

Honey, P. and Mumford, A. (1992) *Manual of Learning Styles*. Maidenhead, Honey: 5–7.

Karasek, Jr. R. A. (1979) Job Demands, Job Decision Latitude and Mental Strain: Implications for Job Redesign. *Administrative Science Quarterly*, 24, June, 285–308.

Karp, H. (1987) The Lost Art of Feedback. In T. W. Pfeiffer (Ed) *Developmental Human Resources*, 237–9.

Kolb, D. (1974) Four styles of managerial learning. In D. Kolb, *et al.* (Eds.) *Organizational Psychology, Book of Readings*, 2nd edn. New York: Prentice Hall International Inc.

Lawrence, G. (1979) *People Types and Tiger Stripes. Practical guide to learning styles*. Florida: Centre for Applications of Psychological Type Inc.

Lazarus, R. S. (1966) *Psychological Stress and the Coping Process*. New York: McGraw-Hill.

Livingston, J. S. (1969) Pygmalion in Management. *Harvard Business Review*, 48, July/August, 81-88.

Luft, J. (1970) *Group Processes: an Introduction to Group Dynamics*. Palo Alto, California: National Press Book.

Luthi, J. Ryck (1978) Communicating Communication. In *Annual Handbook for Group Facilitators*. San Diego, California: Pfeiffer & Co., 123–7.

McCormack, M. (1993) Four forms of persuasion. *'Intercity'* British Rail, London: 49.

McNeil, G. (1993) Pyramid Felling – New Technology will undermine traditional corporate hierarchies. *International Management, October*, 68.

Markham, C. (1993) Insider Dealing. *International Management, December* 56.

Marston, W. M. (1928) *Emotions of Normal People*. Minneapolis: Personal Press Inc.

Maslow, A. H. (1970) *Motivation and Personality*, 2nd ed., New York: Harper & Row.

Mayo, E. (1933) *The Human Problems of an Industrial Civilization*. New York: MacMillan.

O'Connor, J. and Seymour, J. (1990) *Introducing NLP: The new psychology of personal excellence*. Corby: Thorsons Publishing Group.

Pareek, U. and Rao, T. V. (1990) Performance Coaching. In T. W. Pfeiffer (Ed) *Developmental Human Resources*. San Diego, California: Pfeiffer & Co., 249.

Parsloe, E. (1992) *Coaching, Mentoring and Assessing*. London: Kogan Page.

Pfeiffer, J. W. (1993) Conditions which hinder effective communication. *Human Resources Development Abstract*. San Diego, California: Pfeiffer & Co., 120–3.

Reik, T. (1972) *Listening with the Third Ear*. New York: Pyramid Publications.

Salanick, G. and Pfeiffer, S. (1978) A social information processing approach to job attitudes and task design. *Administrative Sciences Quarterly, 25*, 224-253.

Schein, E. H. (1971) The individual, the organisation and the career: a conceptual scheme. *Journal of Applied Behavioural Science, 7*, 401–426.

Sherwood, J. J. and Holyman, F. M. (1978) *Utilizing Human Resources: individual versus group approaches to problem-solving and decision-making*. A handbook for Group Facilitators. San Diego, California: Pfeiffer & Co., 157.

Skinner, B. F. (1953) *Science and Human Behavior*. New York: MacMillan.

Steers, R. M. (1991) *Introduction to Organizational Behavior*, 4th edn. New York: Harper Collins, 79.

Taylor, F. W. (1947) *Scientific Management*. New York: Harper & Row.

Yankelovich (1983) *Work and Human Values*. New York: Public Agenda Foundation.

# FURTHER READING

Argyris, C. (1957) *Personality and Organization*. New York: Harper & Row.

Fontana, D. (1989) *Managing Stress*. London: BPS Books and Routledge.

Hersey, P. and Blanchard, K. (1988) *Management of Organizational Behavior*. New York: Prentice Hall International Inc.

Kennedy, C. (1991) *Guide to Management Gurus*. London: Business Books Ltd.

Likert, R. (1961) *New Patterns of Management*. New York: McGraw-Hill.

McGregor, D. (1960) *The Human Side of Enterprise*. New York: McGraw-Hill

# INDEX:

# Managing Time
## David Fontana

'*a well focused little reader.*'
**NATFHE Journal**

'*There are ideas and suggestions for most of us here ...
very helpful and very useful.*'
**Clinical Psychology Forum**

'*a practical, down to earth book which demonstrates that
psychologists do not live in mumbo-jumbo land.*'
**Training Officer**

Why don't efficiency and successful time-management
always go hand-in-hand? Do you find yourself having
to take work home with you?

By identifying time as 'finite capital' rather than
'renewable income', David Fontana assists readers to:

- clarify aims and objectives
- act rather than re-act
- identify causes of time-wasting
- effectively use technology – and the wastepaper basket
- delegate

Exercises and case studies from different professional
situations are used throughout to help readers identify
and examine unsatisfactory aspects of the way they and
their colleagues, bosses, students and clients manage time.

**Professor David Fontana** is an educational psychologist
with wide experience in running stress- and
time-management workshops.

ISBN: 1 85433 089 6 paperback; 1 85433 088 8 hardback